Behavioral Science & Policy
Volume 3 Issue 2 2017

We welcome new and returning readers to *Behavioral Science & Policy*. This issue presents a new perspective on behavioral nudges, provides original empirical research on savings and on managing technology's risks, and spotlights three reviews on how behavioral insights can guide interventions meant to promote ethical behavior.

In recent years, there has been an explosion of interest in applying insights from behavioral science to the design of policies that promote desired behaviors while preserving freedom of choice—an effort largely inspired by Richard H. Thaler and Cass R. Sunstein's landmark book, *Nudge: Improving Decisions About Health, Wealth, and Happiness*. Much of this work focuses on modifying aspects of the architecture of choice environments; these aspects can include how options are described, how supporting information is presented, the ways people are asked to indicate their preferences or take action, and which option is designated the default. Although choice architecture manipulations frequently succeed, they sometimes fail in surprising ways. In the first article in this issue, Job M. T. Krijnen, David Tannenbaum, and Craig R. Fox argue that policymakers would probably have more success if the traditional notion of choice architecture were updated to account for the relationship between decisionmakers and the choice architect. This relationship plays out in two major ways. First, contextual cues in the choice presentation often prompt decisionmakers to try to discern the beliefs and intentions of the choice architect. Second, decisionmakers may consider the messages that their own behaviors could implicitly communicate to the choice architect and other observers. The article provides ideas that may enable policy designers to anticipate the impact of this "social sensemaking" on the effectiveness of behavioral policy interventions.

A 2016 survey by the Federal Reserve[1] found that nearly half of American adults would not be able to come up with $400 to cover an emergency expense without selling something or borrowing the money. One opportune moment to try to help citizens prepare for such emergencies is when they receive their annual tax refunds; according to the IRS,[2] most American receive refunds averaging a few thousand dollars. Michal Grinstein-Weiss, Cynthia Cryder, Mathieu R. Despard, Dana C. Perantie, Jane E. Oliphant, and Dan Ariely report on a large-scale field experiment administered to low- and moderate-income taxpayers completing their tax returns using TurboTax software. The authors found that by making the option to deposit refunds into a savings account more salient and bolstering this approach with a brief message about the importance of saving, they could substantially increase the tax refund amount that taxpayers directed into savings accounts. In two online follow-up experiments, the authors teased apart the effects of the various intervention elements and found that choice architecture had the greatest impact, but messaging also mattered. Looking at the choice architecture itself, they showed that merely offering the option of directing part of a refund to a savings account was not sufficient to prompt action, whereas offering multiple options that highlighted the option of saving significantly increased the number of refunds and total amount of money directed to savings accounts. Likewise, making it easier for consumers to direct their refunds to savings accounts through a single click increased the number of refunds and total amount of money allocated to savings.

The second empirical report examines how to approach policies for phasing out organizations in high-reliability industries, which are prone to accidents unless a great deal of vigilance is exercised. Markus Schöbel, Ralph Hertwig, and Jörg Rieskamp address, in particular, whether safety risks increase in nuclear plants that are slated to close. The authors explore whether management and employees knowing that a plant is closing leads to the kind of endgame behavior predicted by game theory—that is, to an increase in self-interested behavior as the closure approaches. Using a multimethod approach, the authors first reviewed public records to glean the impact of Germany's 2001 and 2011 announcements of nuclear power phaseouts. They found signs of endgame behavior in public reports of increased stress between utilities and the government. And they found mixed evidence relating to endgame behavior in so-called reportable safety-related events (an increase in these reportable events may imply declines in safety investments). Second, they present two experimental studies in which they found that, largely consistent with predictions of game theory, safety investments increase or stay stable when an end date is uncertain but decrease as a fixed end date approaches. The authors suggest, therefore, that fixed end dates may undermine the goal of safety but that financial incentives explicitly aimed at the maintenance of safety can mitigate problematic endgame patterns.

The financial crisis and several high-profile corporate scandals over the past 10 years or so have led to a crisis of confidence in business ethics. Meanwhile, the behavioral scientific study of ethics, honesty, and morality has made significant advances. This issue closes with three articles that emerged from a 2016 workshop—How to Use Nudges, Norms and Laws to Improve Business Ethics—cohosted by the Behavioral Science & Policy Association and Ethical Systems.

In the first article, Linda K. Treviño, Jonathan Haidt, and Azish E. Filabi synthesize research that can guide efforts to move beyond a traditional check-the-box approach to organizational ethics. After examining current regulatory practices and their effects, they draw on research insights about organizational culture to suggest ways that company leaders can assess their organization's ethical culture and foster a culture that promotes ethical practices.

Next, Nicholas Epley and David Tannenbaum examine ethics as a design problem. They observe that standard policies intended to promote ethical behavior suffer from the misconception that ethics are a property of people (that is, that some people are ethical and others are not) and that good intentions and ethical reasoning are reliable predictors of ethical behavior. The authors draw on social psychology research to suggest instead that ethical or unethical behavior is driven by the situation that a person faces rather than by his or her disposition. With that understanding in mind, they advance several principles to apply when hiring, structuring compensation systems, creating operating principles, and framing an organization's reputation: Highlight ethical issues, because people have limited attention; help people consider an option in terms of whether it is right; and provide incentives for ethical behavior.

Finally, Yuval Feldman examines corruption through a behavioral ethics lens. Consistent with Epley and Tannenbaum's observation that situations rather than dispositions drive unethical behavior, Feldman argues that corruption can arise from vague rules and norms, nonmonetary conflicts of interest, easily available justifications for unethical actions, and organizational loyalty. He also suggests that classical solutions to corruption (such as requiring conflict-of-interest disclosures, requiring multiple approvals, and having formal codes) can actually worsen it by facilitating excuse making for unethical behavior. Instead, he proposes a number of remedies that have been shown to deter people from sliding down the slippery slope toward unethical behavior (such as providing ethical reminders, instituting detection programs, restricting access to potentially prejudicial information, focusing on specific ethical situations, and requiring handwritten declarations).

As always, we hope you find these articles valuable, and we invite your feedback and suggestions as well as submissions of new research findings, essays, and reviews on the applications of behavioral science to policy and practice. Most of all, we look forward to seeing public and private sector policymakers put the practical research described in the pages of this journal to use in service of the public interest.

references

1. Board of Governors of the Federal Reserve System (2017). *Report on the economic well-being of U.S. households in 2016*. Retrieved from https://www.federalreserve.gov/publications/files/2016-report-economic-well-being-us-households-201705.pdf

2. Internal Revenue Service. (2018). Filing season statistics for week ending December 29, 2017. Retrieved from https://www.irs.gov/newsroom/filing-season-statistics-for-week-ending-december-29-2017

Craig R. Fox & Sim B Sitkin
Founding Co-Editors

Choice architecture 2.0: Behavioral policy as an implicit social interaction

Job M. T. Krijnen, David Tannenbaum, & Craig R. Fox

abstract

We propose a new conceptual framework for behavioral policy design that we call *choice architecture 2.0*. We argue that in addition to considering how different choice environments affect decisions (as in conventional choice architecture), choice architects should also be aware of the implicit interaction taking place between the targets of the choice architecture and themselves. When confronting a decision, people often engage in a *social sensemaking* process that entails an assessment of (a) the beliefs and intentions of the choice architect and (b) how their decision will be construed by the choice architect and other observers. We present examples of how this choice architecture 2.0 framework can be used to anticipate factors that moderate the success or failure of behavioral policy interventions, and we provide examples of factors that may trigger social sensemaking. We also present a template for a *social sensemaking audit* that policymakers can perform before implementing any particular design of choice architecture.

Krijnen, J. M. T., Tannenbaum, D., & Fox, C. R. (2017). Choice architecture 2.0: Behavioral policy as an implicit social interaction. *Behavioral Science & Policy, 3*(2), 1–18.

Core Findings

What is the issue?
Behavioral policy design
that employs *choice
architecture* may be
underestimating the
extent to which relevant
decisionmakers engage in
social sensemaking. When
social sensemaking is
triggered, decisionmakers
consider both the
beliefs and intentions
of the choice architect
and how their decision
will be construed by
others. Decisions can
therefore run counter to
intended outcomes.

How can you act?
Selected recommendations
include:
1) Conducting a systematic
social sensemaking audit
before implementing any
choice architecture design
2) Developing and
testing new behavioral
policy tools that take
into account the implicit
interaction between
the choice architect
and decisionmakers

**Who should take
the lead?**
Policymakers acting
as choice architects,
behavioral science
researchers

I n fall 2016, the legislature of the Netherlands wished to increase the percentage of Dutch residents who consented to organ donation. The nation's House of Representatives narrowly passed a highly publicized bill intended to change the donation consent procedure, beginning in 2020, from one requiring explicit consent (an *opt-in* default) to one of presumed consent (an *opt-out* default). Under the policy change, residents would automatically be considered donors unless they returned a letter or went online to elect out of participation. The bill was motivated by recent successes that policymakers around the world have had in applying insights from experimental psychology and behavioral economics to promote better decisions. In particular, policymakers have made gains by modifying *choice architecture*—characteristics of the environment in which options are presented, such as how relevant information is described or how people are asked to indicate their preferences.[1,2]

There are many ways to present choice options to targeted individuals, and the particular presentation can have a large impact on what people decide. Notably, the strategic designation of a favored option as the default has proved to be among the most potent tools available to choice architects. To cite a few examples, employees are more likely to save for retirement when they are automatically enrolled in a 401(k) plan,[3] doctors are more likely to prescribe generic drugs when an electronic health record system automatically replaces branded prescriptions with generic alternatives,[4] and consumers are more likely to receive energy from renewable sources in their homes when they are automatically enrolled in a green rather than a gray energy plan.[5,6] Of particular relevance to the Dutch situation, organ donation consent rates are much higher in European countries where consent is presumed by default compared with countries in which residents must actively elect into donation.[7]

On the basis of these findings, the Dutch legislature made the reasonable assumption that shifting the default designation to one of presumed consent would increase the rate of participation in the donation program.

Remarkably, however, the month after the bill passed the Dutch House of Representatives but before it was ratified into law, the number of residents who registered as nondonors spiked to roughly 40 times the number observed in previous months.[8] (See note A.) This dramatic (albeit temporary) jump in active rejections occurred not only among newly registering residents but also among those who had previously consented to donate and then went to the trouble of revoking their consent.

In fact, the backlash to the Dutch legislature's proposed policy change for organ donation is not without precedent. In the early 1990s, the rates of nonconsent for organ donation rose markedly in Virginia and Texas after these states switched their policies from explicit consent to mandated choice (in which residents are forced to indicate their donation preference when applying for or renewing a driver's license).[9,10] Why did changing defaults in the Netherlands and these U.S. states provoke such strong backlash?

One likely explanation is that some residents may have construed the change (or proposed change) in choice architecture as an attempt at coercion by their government. Residents may have recognized that lawmakers altered policies with the intention of increasing organ donation rates, which provoked many to rebuke that attempt by explicitly opting out. This interpretation suggests that policymakers and behavioral scientists alike need to update their understanding of how choice architecture affects behavior to account for the implicit social interaction taking place between policymakers and targets of behavioral policy.

From Choice Architecture 1.0 to 2.0

When Richard H. Thaler and Cass R. Sunstein coined the term *choice architecture* in their book *Nudge: Improving Decisions About Health, Wealth, and Happiness*, they recognized that individuals targeted by a policy intervention can draw inferences about the intentions of the architects of that policy.[1] For instance, Thaler and Sunstein noted that "in many contexts defaults have some extra nudging power because consumers may feel, rightly or wrongly, that default options come with an implicit endorsement from the default setter, be it the employer, government, or TV scheduler" (p. 35). Since then, however, the insight that choice architecture can also serve a signaling function has not been a central concern of either researchers or policymakers. Thus, the conventional approach to choice architecture (which we might call *choice architecture 1.0*) treats the relationship between the choice architect and the decisionmaker as irrelevant and focuses exclusively on characteristics of the environment in which options are presented.

We propose updating this framework by incorporating an explicit analysis of the implicit social interactions inherent in choice architecture. Our approach, which we call *choice architecture 2.0*, conceives of targeted individuals as "social sensemakers." When confronted with options, individuals will often try to make sense of why

the choice architect has presented the selection in one particular manner rather than in some other arrangement (for example, "Why did my employer set this option as the default?"). Decisionmakers also often care about what their choice reveals to others, including the choice architect. These two sets of issues—what individuals infer about the choice architect and what they think their behavior communicates to others—jointly influence the decisions they make and can determine whether a behavioral policy intervention succeeds or fails. Our approach builds on and complements previous research on topics such as sensemaking in organizations,[11-14] conversational norms that guide everyday language use,[15-17] and contextual inferences.[18-20]

In the remainder of this article, we delve more deeply into the two primary ways that social sensemaking affects responses to a choice architecture (for an overview, see Table 1). First, we present examples of how social

Table 1. Social sensemaking in response to a choice architecture

Stage	Examples of people engaged in social sensemaking	Reference(s)
Information leakage stage (People infer the choice architect's intentions)	*Defaults:* Employees who are more likely to stick with the default retirement plan because they see it as the recommended option.	Brown et al., 2012; McKenzie et al., 2006
	Anchors: Credit card customers who lower their monthly payments in response to the disclosure of minimum repayment information because they interpret the number as a suggested amount.	Keys & Wang, 2014; Navarro-Martinez et al., 2011; Stewart, 2009
	Menu partitions: Health care providers who favor prescribing medications that are listed separately (versus grouped together), potentially because ungrouped treatment options may be viewed as being more commonly prescribed than grouped options.	Tannenbaum et al., 2015; Tannenbaum et al., 2017
	Incentives: Shoppers who bring their own bags because a small surcharge on the use of plastic bags is inferred as communicating social norms about waste reduction.	Lieberman et al., 2017
Behavioral signaling stage (People consider what their choices could communicate to others)	*Defaults:* Residents who assign more social meaning to the act of organ donation if the consent policy in their country is opt in rather than opt out.	Davidai et al., 2012
	Incentives: Female blood donors who infer from the introduction of a monetary reward that their donation would signal self-interest rather than prosocial motives.	Mellström & Johannesson, 2008

inferences about a choice architect's intentions can increase or undermine the effectiveness of a behavioral policy intervention. Second, we expand on the ways that decisionmakers draw inferences about the social ramifications of their own actions and on how those inferences influence the effectiveness of the standard tools of choice architects. Third, we provide a checklist of common factors that can trigger social sensemaking by decisionmakers. Drawing on insights from these three sections, we outline a template for a *social sensemaking audit* that choice architects can perform before implementing any particular design of choice architecture.

We aim our discussion of choice architecture 2.0 at two overlapping audiences. For academic researchers, we highlight factors that can moderate the impact of familiar behavioral policy tools and provide a conceptual framework that may help in the development of new tools. For policymakers, we provide a set of guidelines for anticipating conditions under which the impact of a behavioral policy intervention might be affected by social sensemaking. For both audiences, the updated framework can be thought of as a lens that brings critical features of choice architecture interventions into sharper focus.

Inferences About the Beliefs & Intentions of the Choice Architect (*Information Leakage*)

When do individuals draw inferences about the beliefs and intentions of a choice architect, and why might this matter? A recent empirical finding helps illustrate how this process can play out. In the United States, 401(k) plans have become a popular investment vehicle to help employees save for retirement, partly because employers often contribute additional funds to their workers' accounts. Nevertheless, many eligible employees fail to take full advantage of these plans.[21,22] In 2014, Thaler and Shlomo Benartzi found that providing employees with the option to "save more tomorrow"—by committing in advance to increasing one's retirement contributions upon receiving a future salary raise—boosted both participation

and saving rates.[23] Given the success of this program, it was surprising that in a recent field study by John Beshears and his colleagues, employees given the option to commit to future saving did not increase their participation.[24] In fact, the offer led to a decrease in overall savings contribution rates. Why would seemingly identical interventions increase plan participation in the original studies of Thaler and Benartzi but not in the follow-up study by Beshears and colleagues?

The answer seems to turn on a small but apparently critical difference in the presentation of the options between these studies. Thaler and Benartzi offered employees the "save more tomorrow" option only after employees had already passed up the chance to enroll in a regular 401(k) plan that would have taken effect immediately.[23] Beshears and his collaborators, in contrast, provided employees with a direct choice between initiating saving today versus initiating saving later.[24] Many individuals probably assume that their employer knows more than they do about the urgency of saving for retirement, and employees in the study conducted by Beshears and his colleagues may have inferred that their employer did not consider saving for retirement to be particularly urgent, because the employer offered the option to enroll now or later. Put differently, the choice architects in this latter implementation may have unwittingly leaked information about the (lack of) urgency of retirement saving by how they presented choice options to their employees.[25,26] Indeed, Beshears and his colleagues found support for this hypothesis in a follow-up laboratory experiment. (See note B.)

The manner in which choice architecture communicates or leaks information can take many forms, can be unintentional or by design, and can facilitate or hinder the goals of the choice architect. Next, we provide examples of ways that four common behavioral policy tools can prompt decisionmakers to draw inferences about the choice architect.

Defaults

As discussed in the introduction, choice architects often designate an option as the default consequence if no action is taken by the decisionmaker. One reason defaults are a powerful policy tool is that they can be interpreted by the targeted individual to be the preferred option of the choice architect.[27-29] For instance, it is well-known that participation in retirement saving plans increases when employees are automatically enrolled.[3,30] In one field study, approximately one-third of employees who stayed with the default retirement plan indicated that they did so because they believed it to be the recommended option.[31] Both laboratory and field studies have found that the more a default option is viewed as an implicit recommendation, the more likely people are to stick with that option.[3,28,29]

If decisionmakers distrust the benevolence and competence of a choice architect, however, they will tend to be skeptical of the options the architect appears to endorse. For example, if consumers feel that a choice architect is endorsing an expensive upgrade package merely because the architect wants them to spend more money, consumers will likely reject any upgrade package into which they are automatically enrolled. Indeed, researchers have documented several instances in which defaults selected by distrusted choice architects have failed or backfired, in both laboratory and field settings.[29,32-34]

Anchors

When people make decisions involving numbers, their judgments are often unduly influenced by anchor values provided by the choice architect. For instance, in two experiments, assessments by real estate agents of a home's fair market value were strongly influenced by the putative listing price.[35] Another example involves the minimum-repayment information provided by credit card companies. These disclosures, which indicate the government-mandated minimum amount that consumers would have to repay to avoid a financial charge, were intended to help people avoid amassing unsustainable debt. However, such minimum-repayment values may have served as anchors that were lower than the amount most consumers would have otherwise repaid, inadvertently leading consumers to make lower monthly repayments than would

"information communicated through an anchor can sometimes undermine its intended effect"

have been the case had such minimum repayment amounts never been introduced.[36-38]

One reason why anchors may influence what people choose is that, like defaults, they are sometimes viewed as implicit suggestions being made by the choice architect. That anchors can serve as endorsements might explain why anchoring effects are often stronger when the choice architect is perceived to be more benevolent or more competent. Precise opening offers tend to anchor counteroffers more strongly than imprecise opening offers do, and laboratory studies find that this effect occurs partly because people assume that those making more precise opening offers are more competent. For instance, an opening listing price of $799,812 by a home seller signals that he or she has given greater consideration to the price than a seller who starts with the less precise figure of $800,000. However, this effect can backfire among buyers with greater expertise, who may recognize that a value is unreasonably precise.[39]

As the credit card example suggests, the information communicated through an anchor can sometimes undermine its intended effect. In another illustration, research on charitable giving has found that setting a low amount as the reference (default) donation can lead donors to give less money, on average, than when no reference donation or a high reference donation is set.[40] In online follow-up studies, the downward pull of a low reference donation was stronger when it was presented as a suggested amount than when it was explained that the reference donation was selected at random. A similar dynamic may be relevant to retirement saving. Field research on retirement plan design suggests that although automatic enrollment may increase overall participation, employees may end up saving less money than they otherwise would have (under a nonenrollment default) if their employer's automatic default invests their money in an overly conservative savings plan.[41]

Menu Partitions

Choice architects often partition the list of available options into subsets or groups. For instance, retirement plan sponsors may group available investments by geography (domestic versus international funds), size (small cap versus large cap funds), or risk profile (conservative versus aggressive funds). Studies have found that how the menu space is partitioned can have a pronounced impact on choice, even when the set of available options remains constant, because people are biased toward spreading out their allocations or selections over all identified groups.[42] In fact, the partitioning of options even affects how people decide when choosing a single option. For instance, in one study, medical providers were presented with descriptions of patient symptoms along with a list of possible medications to prescribe.[43] For some providers, the less aggressive medications (for instance, nonprescription medications) were listed separately and all of the more aggressive medications (for instance, prescription medications) were lumped into a single category (labeled *prescription drugs*), whereas other providers saw the opposite menu partition, in which less aggressive medications were grouped into a single category (labeled *over-the-counter drugs*) and the more aggressive medications were listed separately. Medical providers prescribed less aggressive medications more often when those options were listed separately compared with when they were clustered together.

Recent studies suggest that inferences about the popularity of options can sometimes play a role in driving partition dependence.[44] In the absence of explicit information about the rationale for a grouping scheme, decisionmakers may infer that the choice architect grouped options according to how representative or popular those options are. When companies present menus for their products, for example, they often highlight their most popular products

individually and relegate less popular goods to a residual "other products" category. Individuals tend to gravitate toward what is commonly chosen by others,[45] especially when they are uncertain about what to choose, and for this reason may be more apt to select menu items listed separately.

It is worth noting that many past experimental studies investigating partition dependence took pains to rule out information leakage as a necessary driver of the phenomenon,[42,46,47] because these researchers viewed information leakage as an experimental artifact. However, the choice architecture 2.0 framework embraces information leakage as an important factor that contributes to partition dependence and that may generate novel research questions that are especially important to practitioners—for instance, is the size of partitioning effects influenced by whether the decisionmaker trusts the choice architect?

Incentives

Policymakers often introduce financial incentives—rewards or penalties—as a way to promote desired behavior or discourage undesired behavior. The way a financial incentive is presented or structured can exert an influence beyond its monetary value by communicating information about the intentions of the choice architect. For instance, punishments may signal a stronger moral condemnation of unwanted behavior than rewards for good behavior would.[48] In one study, participants learned about a company that introduced either a health insurance premium surcharge for its overweight employees or a premium discount for its healthy-weight employees.[49] Although the financial consequences of the two policies were equivalent, participants inferred that the company held negative attitudes about its overweight employees only when the company introduced a surcharge (that is, a financial penalty). In a follow-up study, participants with higher body mass indices reported they would feel more stigmatized at work and would be more apt to consider looking for employment elsewhere if their employer implemented an overweight penalty than they would

40x

Initial spike in organ nondonor registrants over previous months, once the Dutch parliament passed a mandatory opt-out bill

1/3

Approximate proportion of employees in a field study who indicated that they stayed with the default retirement plan because they believed it to be the recommended option

46%

Decrease in inappropriate antibiotic prescriptions among physicians in an intervention control group who knew their behavior was being observed by researchers if their employer implemented a healthy-weight reward.

Social sensemaking may also explain why imposing a small surcharge on the use of plastic bags in stores is more effective in reducing their usage than offering an equal discount for customers who bring their own bags.[50] This effect appears to stem in part from different inferences made by shoppers about the values held by the choice architect (in this case, the grocery store or the local government).[51] Compared with a discount, a surcharge more strongly communicates to decisionmakers both that the choice architect thinks that customers ought to use their own bags and that most customers do bring their own bags (that is, it suggests that the use of reusable bags conforms with both injunctive and descriptive social norms).

Beyond the framing of an incentive, the mere introduction of a reward or punishment may be interpreted by decisionmakers as a sign of the choice architect's view about the attractiveness or unattractiveness of a behavior.[52,53] For instance, one study found that residents of two Swiss communities were less likely to accept the building of a nuclear waste facility near their homes when they were offered financial compensation.[54] Presumably, residents inferred from the offer of compensation that having a nuclear waste facility nearby was especially hazardous or unappealing.

Inferences About the Social Meaning of the Decisionmaker's Own Behavior (*Behavioral Signaling*)

Gleaning the intent of the choice architect can be thought of as the first stage of social sensemaking by decisionmakers. This is sometimes followed by a second stage where decisionmakers infer what their own behavior signals to the choice architect and other potential observers.

A clear example of this second form of sensemaking comes from a study that tested an approach to reducing the profligate prescribing

of antibiotics by U.S. clinicians; such over-prescribing contributes to the evolution of antibiotic-resistant superbugs.[55,56] In 2016, Daniella Meeker and her colleagues found that two interventions led to dramatic decreases in inappropriate prescribing for nonbacterial upper respiratory infections: (a) prompting physicians via the electronic health record system to write a justification for each dubious prescription, which reduced inappropriate prescribing from 23% of the time to 5% of the time, and (b) providing physicians with monthly e-mails comparing their inappropriate prescription rates with those of top performers—doctors with the lowest rates—in their region, which reduced inappropriate prescribing from 20% of the time to 4% of the time.[57] There is, however, a remarkable sidenote to this success story. It turns out that clinicians in the control condition—who received no intervention beyond a bland education module that taught nothing they did not already know—also reduced their inappropriate antibiotic prescribing substantially over the course of the study, from 24% of the time to 13% of the time (a 46% decrease). It seems unlikely that the education module was responsible for this reduction, as it presented little that was new and previous educational interventions have not been particularly effective in reducing antibiotics prescription rates.[58] So why would enrollment in a control condition have such a strong impact on prescribing behavior?

Choice architecture 2.0 refocuses attention on what might otherwise be seen as an experimental artifact. It seems plausible that many clinicians, knowing that their prescribing behavior would be monitored by researchers from several prestigious institutions, adjusted their behavior so they would be seen in the best possible light by these choice architects. Indeed, consistent with this notion, the most precipitous reduction in inappropriate antibiotic prescribing among physicians in the control group occurred at the very beginning of the intervention, and the effect persisted throughout the intervention period. (See note C.)

In fact, pronounced improvement in the behavior of participants in the control condition of field interventions is not an uncommon

"people may actively resist persuasion attempts or react against threats to their freedom to choose"

observation. When conducting field studies, researchers frequently find that participants behave in a more socially desirable manner when they are aware that their actions are being monitored, a pattern often called a *Hawthorne effect*.[59] (See note D.) For instance, a recent study showed that airline captains made more effective decisions about the amount of fuel to carry onboard after simply learning that they were being observed by investigators—the intended control condition of a larger study on the impact of incentives.[60] Other research found that households reduced the amount of electricity they used after being notified that they had been selected to participate in a study on electricity usage.[61] Researchers typically view the Hawthorne effect as an empirical nuisance that challenges their ability to assess the independent influences of experimental interventions that are of greater theoretical interest.[59,62] From a choice architecture 2.0 perspective, however, the Hawthorne effect can serve as a potent and cost-effective tool for changing behavior.

The Hawthorne effect belongs to a broader family of behavioral responses to being observed. An abundance of research has found that decisionmakers tend to be concerned with the social meaning of their actions and often shift toward more socially desirable behavior when they are made to feel accountable to observers. For instance, one study found that promising to publish neighborhood voting records (indicating who voted and who did not) increased turnout in Michigan's 2006 primary election.[63] In addition, a vast literature suggests that feeling accountable or worrying about one's reputation becomes more salient when decisionmakers expect that the choice architect will ask them to provide justification for their choices.[64]

In some contexts, a decisionmaker's desire to be viewed in a positive light may be trumped by a reaction against the perceived intrusion of a choice architect. A long line of research has established that, to maintain and protect control over their own lives, people may actively resist persuasion attempts[65] or react against threats to their freedom to choose.[66-68] If decisionmakers perceive a choice architecture to be coercive or a threat to their autonomy, they may be moved to demonstrate their independence by behaving contrary to what they surmise to be the choice architect's goal—as was observed in the previously mentioned case of organ consent defaults in the Netherlands, Virginia, and Texas. We suspect that such reactance is particularly likely to occur in situations that are personally consequential (such as when deciding whether to be an organ donor),[67] among individuals who are especially concerned about their sense of freedom,[69] and when the choice architect is distrusted.[29,70]

The preceding analysis shows that inferences about how one's actions may be evaluated by a choice architect and other potential observers can alter behavior, a phenomenon that could be harnessed intentionally as its own independent tool of behavioral policy. Additionally, such inferences may increase or decrease the effectiveness of familiar behavioral policy tools, as we illustrate next.

Defaults

A choice architect's decision to designate participation or nonparticipation in an organ donation program as the default may not only communicate information from the choice architect to the decisionmaker but may also affect the meaning that decisionmakers attach to their own choices. For instance, Germany has much lower consent rates for organ donation (12%) than does neighboring Austria (virtually 100%), a difference that is commonly attributed to Germany having an explicit consent (opt-in) default, whereas Austria has a presumed consent (opt-out) default.[7] Research finds that Germans assign greater meaning to the act of organ donation than do Austrians, despite strong cultural similarities between the two countries.[71]

A follow-up experiment provides more direct evidence that the default regime affects the meaning attached to different choices. American participants read about a country with either an opt-in or an opt-out organ donation policy and then rated the extent to which they would view organ donation under the given policy as an act of self-sacrifice relative to other prosocial behaviors. Participants who read about the country with an opt-in policy rated the act of organ donation as being comparable to self-sacrificing acts such as bequeathing one's wealth to charity. In contrast, participants who read about the country with an opt-out policy rated the act of organ donation as less significant, comparable to polite behaviors such as letting another person go ahead in line.

Concerns about how decisionmakers will be viewed by others are especially influential when the choices made would signal sensitive or stigmatizing information. For instance, in one study, participants were given the opportunity to test for a fictitious disease that they had read about during a previous study session.[72] Some participants learned that the disease was contracted via unprotected sex (a socially stigmatized behavior), whereas others learned that the disease was spread by coughing or sneezing. The option to test for the disease was presented to participants as either opt in (in which testing is voluntary) or opt out (in which testing is routine but the individual can choose to forgo it). The default intervention had greater impact when testing involved a disease with potentially stigmatizing implications. Apparently, participants were more reluctant to opt into voluntary testing for the stigmatized disease because of what their choice might reveal ("Getting tested may tell others that I've engaged in risky behaviors and have something to worry about"). For similar reasons, participants were also more reluctant to opt out of routine testing for the stigmatized disease ("Not getting tested may make it look like I have something to hide").

Incentives
Whether an incentive is framed as a reward or a punishment can affect decisionmakers' expectations of how others will judge them.[73] As a result, well-meaning incentives can sometimes backfire.[53,74,75] Consider a well-known study conducted at an Israeli day care center. In an attempt to get parents to pick up their children on time, the school introduced a small fine for tardiness. In fact, the penalty had the opposite of the intended effect—it led to an increase in lateness.[76] The researchers speculated that introducing a fine might have changed how parents thought their behavior would be perceived by the employees of the day care center. Before the introduction of the fine, showing up late may have been perceived as a moral violation (or perhaps as evidence of bad parenting). After the introduction of the fine, showing up late may have been perceived as merely a financial transaction. That is, many parents may have construed the small fine as a price rather than a penalty so that, ironically, this financial disincentive now allowed them to feel unembarrassed about taking advantage of additional child care.

Social sensemaking can also modify the effectiveness of rewards designed to promote prosocial behavior. For instance, one study found that women (although not men) were less likely to donate blood when a monetary reward was introduced.[77] This pattern of results suggests that the women cared about the social meaning of their actions: presumably, they inferred from the introduction of the monetary reward that their blood donation could be perceived as being motivated by self-interest. Consistent with this interpretation, the rate of blood donations among women did not decline when participants were given the option to donate the money to a charity, probably because donation of the reward eliminated the potential appearance of self-interest.

Triggers of Social Sensemaking
Although all decisions are made in settings characterized by a particular choice architecture,[78] we do not suggest that decisionmakers always engage in social sensemaking. Some forms of social sensemaking are more deliberate, whereas others are more intuitive; further, some conditions provide more mental bandwidth for social sensemaking than others (such as when people are less rushed or distracted), and some

individuals may have a greater tendency to engage in such thinking than others.

For now, we assert that several situational factors are likely to trigger social sensemaking by decisionmakers and that choice architects can design more effective interventions if they keep these triggers in mind. In Figure 1, we provide a checklist with questions that, when answered affirmatively, could be used to determine whether choice architecture 2.0 thinking is especially called for in the design, implementation, or calibration of behavioral policy interventions. These five questions can be remembered using the acronym PreDICT.

Preference Uncertainty: Are Decisionmakers Uncertain About Their Preferences?

Decisionmakers who are unsure about how to decide may actively search for guiding cues from the way the options are presented. This tendency may partly explain why defaults in retirement saving have a greater impact on people with little financial knowledge[33] or why ballot order has a greater effect on voters who have little information available.[79] Similarly, people may be more receptive to perceived guidance from choice architects when they subjectively feel that they lack relevant knowledge (regardless of whether they objectively lack such knowledge).[80] Indeed, a recent series of laboratory studies involving investment decisions found that people who were made to feel less knowledgeable were more receptive to adopting the default retirement saving option.[81]

Distrust: Are Decisionmakers Suspicious of the Choice Architect?

As alluded to earlier, distrust of the choice architect may lead a decisionmaker to actively consider the choice architect's beliefs and intentions. Such questioning may, in turn, reduce the effectiveness of many policy interventions. Studies find that decisionmakers are more disapproving of behavioral interventions when they are implemented by choice architects whom they oppose politically[82] or perceive as dishonest.[83] This propensity may explain why one field experiment found that households in more politically conservative counties were more resistant to a "green nudge" intended to promote energy conservation—a monthly energy report with personalized information about electricity usage over time and a comparison to the electricity usage of neighbors.[84] We also suspect that regional differences in trust in government could be one factor explaining geographic variation in the level of public acceptance of behavioral policy interventions.[85]

Past experiences with a particular choice architect may affect decisionmakers' subsequent level of trust in the architect, which may, in turn, influence the impact of the associated choice architecture. Thus, responses to choice architecture may sometimes be construed as a repeated social interaction in which both parties learn over time and may even (strategically) adjust their actions.[86] For instance, an insurance company implementing default insurance plans tailored to the characteristics and preferences of each customer (which have been called *smart defaults*)[87] may improve the satisfaction of their customers. This satisfaction may lead those same customers to place greater trust in the company and make them more willing to rely on defaults selected by the same choice architect in the future.

Importance: Is the Decision Especially Meaningful to Decisionmakers?

People are prone to process information more carefully when the issue at hand is more

Figure 1. PreDICT checklist

A yes answer to any of the questions below signifies that the choice architecture is especially likely to trigger social sensemaking by decisionmakers.

✓ **Pre**ference uncertainty	Are decisionmakers uncertain about their preferences?
✓ **D**istrust	Are decisionmakers suspicious of the choice architect?
✓ **I**mportance	Is the decision especially meaningful to decisionmakers?
✓ **C**hange	Is the choice architecture noticeably different or abnormal?
✓ **T**ransparency	Is the strategic modification of choice architecture explicitly communicated to decisionmakers?

important to them.[88-90] We suspect, therefore, that decisionmakers are more likely to consider the beliefs and intentions of a choice architect when the decision is more personally relevant or important. For instance, employees are probably more apt to evaluate their employer's rationale for selecting a particular option as the default when the issue at hand is investments offered in a company retirement saving program versus something relatively trivial, such as the font used in company e-mails.

Change: Is the Choice Architecture Noticeably Different or Abnormal?

People are more likely to draw causal inferences when they find a situation unusual or unexpected.[88,91-94] We therefore presume that decisionmakers are more likely to engage in social sensemaking when they recognize that a presentation of options has changed or is about to change. For instance, most Dutch residents probably engaged in more social sensemaking about organ donation defaults after the Dutch legislature proposed a highly publicized change to the default than they did before the proposal. When sensemaking is triggered by a change in choice architecture, people may gradually come to regard the new policy as normal and subsequently be less likely to engage in sensemaking as time goes on.

Transparency: Is the Strategic Modification of Choice Architecture Explicitly Communicated to Decisionmakers?

It may seem obvious that people are more likely to engage in social sensemaking when the design of a choice architecture is explicitly pointed out to them. A choice architecture 2.0 lens not only suggests that transparency will tend to trigger social sensemaking but also helps identify how transparency is likely to affect the success of a policy intervention. On the one hand, studies on resistance to persuasion suggest that when transparency highlights the choice architect's intention to nudge behavior, decisionmakers may shift their attitudes (and therefore choices) in the opposite direction.[95,96] On the other hand, many have argued that being transparent about the goals and motives underlying the selection of a particular choice architecture is more ethical and makes the

"People are more likely to draw causal inferences when they find a situation unusual or unexpected"

approach more acceptable to the public;[97-99] such honesty has also been found to reduce skepticism, increase perceived fairness, and engender trust.[83,100] A third possibility is that transparency can sometimes have a minimal impact on the effectiveness of choice architecture interventions: Recent studies have found that default effects did not diminish even when choice architects were transparent about the typical impact that defaults have on people's decisions.[100-103] Although further research is needed, it appears that in at least some contexts, policymakers can promote transparency without sacrificing the effectiveness of choice architecture interventions. (See note E.)

Conclusion: Introducing the Social Sensemaking Audit

The impact of choice architecture on decisions is not always easy to anticipate. In this article, we have proposed an updated conception of choice architecture—from 1.0 to 2.0—that enhances the traditional framework by treating the implicit interaction between decisionmakers and the choice architect as a crucial factor to be considered in the crafting of effective behavioral policy. Decisionmakers often seek information about the beliefs and intentions of the choice architect; they also infer what their own behavior may communicate to the choice architect and other observers. This updated perspective can help policymakers and behavioral researchers in the design and implementation of more effective choice architecture interventions by highlighting the importance of seemingly irrelevant implementation details that may influence the success of an intervention. A choice architecture 2.0 perspective also points to the development of new tools of behavioral policy, such as explicitly informing decisionmakers that their behavior is being monitored (that is, leveraging the Hawthorne effect deliberately to prompt more mindful behavior).

As previewed in the introduction of this article, a choice architecture 2.0 framework suggests that policymakers should routinely engage in a social sensemaking audit before finalizing the design of a particular choice architecture (see Figure 2). The major elements of such an audit can be summarized as follows. First, choice architects ought to ask to what extent social sensemaking is likely to be triggered. Second, if social sensemaking seems likely, then ask what decisionmakers might infer about the intentions and beliefs of the choice architect and to what extent decisionmakers would find the choice architect competent and benevolent. For instance, a nudge that appears to be an endorsement may be more influential if decisionmakers feel the choice architect has their best interests in mind and is capable of identifying the best option for them. Third, if social sensemaking is likely, choice architects ought to consider what decisionmakers could assume their choices would signal to observers. Again, decisionmakers' relationship with the choice architect will be key to anticipating how this reverse information leakage is likely to affect decisionmakers' choices. For instance, decisionmakers are likely to behave in socially desirable ways to the extent that the choice architect's or other observers' evaluations are valued and the decisionmakers know that their choices are personally identifiable. This social sensemaking audit may lead choice architects to consider making triggers more or less salient, communicating their beliefs and intentions explicitly to forestall faulty inferences by decisionmakers, cultivating a greater degree of trust with targeted decisionmakers, or taking an entirely different approach to the design of choice architecture than the one originally considered.

The possibility of social sensemaking—typically neglected by practitioners applying a conventional approach to choice architecture—is another reason why practitioners ought to, whenever possible, test interventions in the field before scaling them up.[104] Choice architects should be especially wary of proceeding without testing if the common sensemaking triggers outlined in Figure 1 are present. When pilot testing any potential choice architecture implementation, policymakers could explicitly probe for sensemaking inferences and concerns and incorporate this feedback into the design before finalizing and scaling up the policy.

Figure 2. A template for a social sensemaking audit

Choice architects should ask themselves the questions in this figure before implementing any particular choice architecture design.

Step 1: Triggers
Is social sensemaking likely to be triggered?
See Figure 1 for the PreDICT checklist.

↓

Step 2: Information Leakage
What might decisionmakers infer about the beliefs and intentions of the choice architect?
What are the decisionmaker's feelings toward the choice architect?
For instance, does the decisionmaker trust or distrust the choice architect?

↓

Step 3: Behavioral Signaling
To what extent do decisionmakers feel that their behavior will be observed by others?
What do decisionmakers think is the social meaning of this behavior?

We conclude by highlighting a final use of the social sensemaking audit: to properly diagnose why a particular implementation of choice architecture did not work as intended so that these insights can be incorporated into future launches. To illustrate, we return to the Dutch case of sharply increased withdrawal of organ donation consent after a proposed change in the default regime. (See note F.) What can one learn in hindsight by performing a three-step social sensemaking audit? First, it seems that Dutch residents were triggered to engage in social sensemaking by the abundant publicity given to the bill and by the fact that many viewed decisions about organ donation as personally important. Second, these factors likely prompted Dutch residents to assess the intention behind the policy—namely, that policymakers were attempting to increase consent rates for organ donation. Although some Dutch residents may have been positively influenced by this implicit endorsement, others probably reacted against a perceived attempt to manipulate them, especially if they distrusted their legislators. Third, many of these indignant residents may have considered opting out to be an act of protest carrying social meaning that would be observed (at least in aggregate) by legislators and the public, enabling them to signal their displeasure. Consistent with this interpretation, many Dutch residents publicly shared their decisions to opt out through social media.[105–107]

Had the legislators anticipated this response, they might have taken steps to preempt the backlash, such as by more carefully managing communication about the proposed policy change and pilot testing its implementation. For instance, rather than speaking about the ways that changing to an opt-out default would nudge more residents to become organ donors, legislators might have emphasized other benefits for the public. They could have noted, for example, that a large proportion of Dutch residents wished to become potential organ donors and that the bill was designed to reduce obstacles to achieving that desired aim. Such an approach might have been more successful for two reasons. First, it signals a descriptive social norm (many Dutch residents prefer to be potential donors) toward which people may gravitate. Second, it potentially reduces negative reactions by framing the policy change as one designed to help residents express their preferences rather than one that coerces them to do something that the legislature deems desirable.

Of course, the foregoing analysis is speculative and would need to be confirmed empirically. More generally, we hope that the choice architecture 2.0 perspective advanced in this article will inspire a fruitful stream of research that more fully fleshes out the relationship between social sensemaking by decisionmakers and the effectiveness of behavioral policy interventions. In addition, we hope that this framework will help practitioners who are designing and evaluating choice architecture in the field to focus on the implementation details that are most critical to the success of behavioral policy interventions.

author affiliation

Krijnen: University of California, Los Angeles. Tannenbaum: University of Utah. Fox: University of California, Los Angeles. Corresponding author's e-mail: job.krijnen@anderson.ucla.edu.

author note

An earlier version of ideas contained in this article was presented by Fox at the August 2016 Academy of Management Conference in Anaheim, California. We thank Alain Cohn, Hengchen Dai, Jana Gallus, Jon Jachimowicz, Dean Karlan, Alicea Lieberman, and Stephen Spiller for helpful comments on earlier drafts of this article.

endnotes

A. This number was corroborated by a personal communication from the Dutch agency registering organ donation consent (*Agentschap CIBG—Donorregister*), received June 1, 2017.

B. It is worth noting that Beshears et al. (in the study provided in reference 24) tested their explanation in a laboratory setting, which may have exacerbated the social concerns of participants relative to the field experiment.

C. This is not apparent from the published version of the article cited in reference 57, which provides smoothed data, but it can be seen from the raw data, which are available from the authors of that article upon request.

D. This pattern is called a *Hawthorne effect* because it was first noted in studies from the 1920s and 1930s at the Hawthorne Works (a Western Electric factory) outside Chicago. The studies reported that experimentally manipulated changes in working conditions (for example, the brightness of lighting) led to increases in worker productivity, regardless of the nature of those changes, but these improvements diminished after the study ended and workers were no longer reminded that they were being observed. The original data from the interventions at the Hawthorne plant were analyzed in a 2011 article (see reference 59), and the authors concluded that "ironically, there is little evidence of the type of Hawthorne effect widely attributed to these data when one subjects them to careful analysis."

E. For a related discussion on the effects that different forms of transparency may have, see "Putting the Public Back in Behavioral Public Policy," by P. De Jonge, M. Zeelenberg, and P. W. J. Verlegh, *Behavioural Public Policy,* in press.

F. We hasten to point out that the backlash in the Netherlands was temporary. In the months after the bill was passed, the rate of new nondonors slowly returned to the rate at which it had been before. Although it is quite likely that in the long run the introduction of an opt-out system will have a positive effect on the number of people who consent to organ donation, it still would have been better if the Dutch legislature had been able to prevent the backlash altogether.

references

1. Thaler, R. H., & Sunstein, C. R. (2008). *Nudge: Improving decisions about health, wealth, and happiness.* New Haven, CT: Yale University Press.

2. Johnson, E. J., Shu, S., Dellaert, B., Fox, C., Goldstein, D., Häubl, G., & Weber, E. (2012). Beyond nudges: Tools of a choice architecture. *Marketing Letters, 23,* 487–504.

3. Madrian, B. C., & Shea, D. F. (2001). The power of suggestion: Inertia in 401(k) participation and savings behavior. *Quarterly Journal of Economics, 116,* 1149–1187.

4. Malhotra, S., Cheriff, A. D., Gossey, J. T., Cole, C. L., Kaushal, R., & Ancker, J. S. (2016). Effects of an e-prescribing interface redesign on rates of generic drug prescribing: Exploiting default options. *Journal of the American Medical Informatics Association, 23,* 891–898.

5. Ebeling, F., & Lotz, S. (2015). Domestic uptake of green energy promoted by opt-out tariffs. *Nature Climate Change, 5,* 868–871.

6. Pichert, D., & Katsikopoulos, K. V. (2008). Green defaults: Information presentation and pro-environmental behaviour. *Journal of Environmental Psychology, 28,* 63–73.

7. Johnson, E. J., & Goldstein, D. (2003, November 21). Do defaults save lives? *Science, 302,* 1338–1339.

8. Centraal Bureau voor de Statistiek. (2017, July 26). Ontwikkelingen donorregistraties 2016 [Developments donor registrations 2016]. Retrieved from https://www.cbs.nl/nl-nl/nieuws/2017/30/ontwikkeling-donorregistraties-2016

9. August, J. G. (2013). Modern models of organ donation: Challenging increases of federal power to save lives. *Hastings Constitutional Law Quarterly, 40,* 339–422.

10. Siminoff, L. A., & Mercer, M. B. (2001). Public policy, public opinion, and consent for organ donation. *Cambridge Quarterly of Healthcare Ethics, 10,* 377–386.

11. Maitlis, S. (2005). The social processes of organizational sensemaking. *Academy of Management Journal, 48,* 21–49.

12. Maitlis, S., & Christianson, M. (2014). Sensemaking in organizations: Taking stock and moving forward. *Academy of Management Annals, 8,* 57–125.

13. Weick, K. (1995). *Sensemaking in organizations.* London, United Kingdom: Sage.

14. Weick, K. E., Sutcliffe, K. M., & Obstfeld, D. (2005). Organizing and the process of sensemaking. *Organization Science, 16,* 409–421.

15. Grice, H. P. (1975). Logic and conversation. In P. Cole & N. L. Morgan (Eds.), *Syntax and semantics: Speech acts* (Vol. 3, pp. 41–58). New York, NY: Academic Press.

16. Orne, M. T. (1962). On the social psychology of the psychological experiment: With particular reference to demand characteristics and their implications. *American Psychologist, 17,* 776–783.

17. Schwarz, N. (1994). Judgment in a social context: Biases, shortcomings, and the logic of conversation. *Advances in Experimental Social Psychology, 26,* 123–162.

18. Kamenica, E. (2008). Contextual inference in markets: On the informational content of product lines. *American Economic Review, 98,* 2127–2149.

19. Prelec, D., Wernerfelt, B., & Zettelmeyer, F. (1997). The role of inference in context effects: Inferring what you want from what is available. *Journal of Consumer Research, 24,* 118–125.

20. Wernerfelt, B. (1995). A rational reconstruction of the compromise effect: Using market data to infer utilities. *Journal of Consumer Research, 21,* 627–633.

21. Choi, J. J., Laibson, D., & Madrian, B. C. (2011). $100 bills on the sidewalk: Suboptimal investment in 401(k) plans. *Review of Economics and Statistics, 93,* 748–763.

22. Rhee, N. (2013). *The retirement savings crisis: Is it worse than we think?* Washington, DC: National Institute on Retirement Security.

23. Thaler, R. H., & Benartzi, S. (2004). Save More Tomorrow™: Using behavioral economics to increase employee saving. *Journal of Political Economy, 112,* 164–187.

24. Beshears, J., Dai, H., Milkman, K. L., & Benartzi, S. (2017). *Framing the future: The risks of pre-commitment nudges and potential of fresh start messaging.* Working paper.

25. McKenzie, C. R., & Nelson, J. D. (2003). What a speaker's choice of frame reveals: Reference points, frame selection, and framing effects. *Psychonomic Bulletin & Review, 10,* 596–602.

26. Sher, S., & McKenzie, C. R. (2006). Information leakage from logically equivalent frames. *Cognition, 101,* 467–494.

27. Jachimowicz, J. M., Duncan, S., & Weber, E. U. (2017). *When and why defaults influence decisions: A meta-analysis of default effects.* Working paper.

28. McKenzie, C. R., Liersch, M. J., & Finkelstein, S. R. (2006). Recommendations implicit in policy defaults. *Psychological Science, 17,* 414–420.

29. Tannenbaum, D., & Ditto, P. H. (2011). *Information asymmetries in default options.* Working paper.

30. Beshears, J., Choi, J. J., Laibson, D., & Madrian, B. C. (2009). The importance of default options for retirement saving outcomes: Evidence from the United States. In J. Brown, J. B. Liebman, & D. A. Wise (Eds.), *Social Security policy in a changing environment* (pp. 167–195). Chicago, IL: University of Chicago Press.

31. Brown, J. R., Farrell, A. M., & Weisbenner, S. J. (2012). *The downside of defaults.* Retrieved from http://www.nber.org/aging/rrc/papers/orrc12-05.pdf

32. Liersch, M. J., & McKenzie, C. R. M. (2009). *In defaults we trust.* Unpublished manuscript.

33. Agnew, J. R., & Szykman, L. R. (2005). Asset allocation and information overload: The influence of information display, asset choice, and investor experience. *Journal of Behavioral Finance, 6,* 57–70.

34. Brown, C. L., & Krishna, A. (2004). The skeptical shopper: A metacognitive account for the effects of default options on choice. *Journal of Consumer Research, 31,* 529–539.

35. Northcraft, G. B., & Neale, M. A. (1987). Experts, amateurs, and real estate: An anchoring-and-adjustment perspective on property pricing decisions. *Organizational Behavior and Human Decision Processes, 39,* 84–97.

36. Keys, B. J., & Wang, J. (2014). *Perverse nudges: Minimum payments and debt paydown in consumer credit cards* [Working paper]. Retrieved from https://www.economicdynamics.org/meetpapers/2014/paper_323.pdf

37. Navarro-Martinez, D., Salisbury, L. C., Lemon, K. N., Stewart, N., Matthews, W. J., & Harris, A. J. (2011). Minimum

required payment and supplemental information disclosure effects on consumer debt repayment decisions. *Journal of Marketing Research, 48,* S60–S77.

38. Stewart, N. (2009). The cost of anchoring on credit-card minimum repayments. *Psychological Science, 20,* 39–41.

39. Loschelder, D. D., Friese, M., Schaerer, M., & Galinsky, A. D. (2016). The too-much-precision effect: When and why precise anchors backfire with experts. *Psychological Science, 27,* 1573–1587.

40. Goswami, I., & Urminsky, O. (2016). When should the ask be a nudge? The effect of default amounts on charitable donations. *Journal of Marketing Research, 53,* 829–846.

41. Choi, J. J., Laibson, D., Madrian, B. C., & Metrick, A. (2004). For better or for worse: Default effects and 401(k) savings behavior. In D. A. Wise (Ed.), *Perspectives on the economics of aging* (pp. 81–126). Chicago, IL: University of Chicago Press.

42. Fox, C. R., Ratner, R. K., & Lieb, D. S. (2005). How subjective grouping of options influences choice and allocation: Diversification bias and the phenomenon of partition dependence. *Journal of Experimental Psychology: General, 134,* 538–551.

43. Tannenbaum, D., Doctor, J. N., Persell, S. D., Friedberg, M. W., Meeker, D., Friesema, E. M., . . . Fox, C. R. (2015). Nudging physician prescription decisions by partitioning the order set: Results of a vignette-based study. *Journal of General Internal Medicine, 30,* 298–304.

44. Tannenbaum, D., Fox, C. R., & Goldstein, N. J. (2017). *Partitioning menu items to nudge single-item choice* [Working paper]. Retrieved from https://davetannenbaum.github.io/documents/pdepend.pdf

45. Cialdini, R. B., Kallgren, C. A., & Reno, R. R. (1991). A focus theory of normative conduct: A theoretical refinement and reevaluation of the role of norms in human behavior. *Advances in Experimental Social Psychology, 24,* 201–234.

46. Fox, C. R., & Clemen, R. T. (2005). Subjective probability assessment in decision analysis: Partition dependence and bias toward the ignorance prior. *Management Science, 51,* 1417–1432.

47. Sonnemann, U., Camerer, C. F., Fox, C. R., & Langer, T. (2013). How psychological framing affects economic market prices in the lab and field. *Proceedings of the National Academy of Sciences, USA, 110,* 11779–11784.

48. Mulder, L. B. (2008). The difference between punishments and rewards in fostering moral concerns in social decision making. *Journal of Experimental Social Psychology, 44,* 1436–1443.

49. Tannenbaum, D., Valasek, C. J., Knowles, E. D., & Ditto, P. H. (2013). Incentivizing wellness in the workplace: Sticks (not carrots) send stigmatizing signals. *Psychological Science, 24,* 1512–1522.

50. Homonoff, T. A. (2015). *Can small incentives have large effects? The impact of taxes versus bonuses on disposable bag use.* Working paper.

51. Lieberman, A. J., Duke, K., & Amir, O. (2017). *How incentive framing can harness the power of social norms.* Working paper.

52. Bénabou, R., & Tirole, J. (2003). Intrinsic and extrinsic motivation. *Review of Economic Studies, 70,* 489–520.

53. Bowles, S. (2008, June 20). Policies designed for self-interested citizens may undermine "the moral sentiments": Evidence from economic experiments. *Science, 320,* 1605–1609.

54. Frey, B. S., & Oberholzer-Gee, F. (1997). The cost of price incentives: An empirical analysis of motivation crowding-out. *American Economic Review, 87,* 746–755.

55. Exec. Order No. 13676, 3 C.F.R. 56931 (2014). *Combating antibiotic-resistant bacteria.* Retrieved from https://www.whitehouse.gov/the-press-office/2014/09/18/executive-order-combating-antibiotic-resistant-bacteria

56. Review on Antimicrobial Resistance. (2016). *Tackling drug-resistant infections globally: Final report and recommendations.* Retrieved from https://amr-review.org/sites/default/files/160518_Final%20paper_with%20cover.pdf

57. Meeker, D., Linder, J. A., Fox, C. R., Friedberg, M. W., Persell, S. D., Goldstein, N. J., . . . Doctor, J. N. (2016). Effect of behavioral interventions on inappropriate antibiotic prescribing among primary care practices: A randomized clinical trial. *JAMA, 315,* 562–570.

58. Barnett, M. L., & Linder, J. A. (2014). Antibiotic prescribing for adults with acute bronchitis in the United States, 1996–2010. *JAMA, 311,* 2020–2022.

59. Levitt, S. D., & List, J. A. (2011). Was there really a Hawthorne effect at the Hawthorne plant? An analysis of the original illumination experiments. *American Economic Journal: Applied Economics, 3,* 224–238.

60. Gosnell, G. K., List, J. A., & Metcalfe, R. (2016). *A new approach to an age-old problem: Solving externalities by incenting workers directly* (NBER Working Paper No. 22316). Cambridge, MA: National Bureau of Economic Research.

61. Schwartz, D., Fischhoff, B., Krishnamurti, T., & Sowell, F. (2013). The Hawthorne effect and energy awareness. *Proceedings of the National Academy of Sciences, USA, 110,* 15242–15246.

62. Zizzo, D. J. (2010). Experimenter demand effects in economic experiments. *Experimental Economics, 13,* 75–98.

63. Gerber, A. S., Green, D. P., & Larimer, C. W. (2008). Social pressure and voter turnout: Evidence from a large-scale field experiment. *American Political Science Review, 102,* 33–48.

64. Lerner, J. S., & Tetlock, P. E. (1999). Accounting for the effects of accountability. *Psychological Bulletin, 125,* 255–275.

65. Friestad, M., & Wright, P. (1994). The persuasion knowledge model: How people cope with persuasion attempts. *Journal of Consumer Research, 21,* 1–31.

66. Brehm, J. W. (1966). *A theory of psychological reactance.* Oxford, United Kingdom: Academic Press.

67. Clee, M. A., & Wicklund, R. A. (1980). Consumer behavior and psychological reactance. *Journal of Consumer Research, 6,* 389–405.

68. Wicklund, R. A. (1974). *Freedom and reactance.* Oxford, United Kingdom: Erlbaum.

69. Jung, J. Y., & Mellers, B. A. (2016). American attitudes toward nudges. *Judgment and Decision Making, 11,* 62–74.

70. Agnew, J. R., Szykman, L. R., Utkus, S. P., & Young, J. A. (2012). Trust, plan knowledge and 401(k) savings behavior. *Journal of Pension Economics & Finance, 11,* 1–20.

71. Davidai, S., Gilovich, T., & Ross, L. D. (2012). The meaning of default options for potential organ donors. *Proceedings*

of the National Academy of Sciences, USA, 109, 15201–15205.

72. Young, S. D., Monin, B., & Owens, D. (2009). Opt-out testing for stigmatized diseases: A social psychological approach to understanding the potential effect of recommendations for routine HIV testing. Health Psychology, 28, 675–681.

73. Bénabou, R., & Tirole, J. (2006). Incentives and prosocial behavior. American Economic Review, 96, 1652–1678.

74. Kamenica, E. (2012). Behavioral economics and psychology of incentives. Annual Review of Economics, 4, 427–452.

75. Gneezy, U., Meier, S., & Rey-Biel, P. (2011). When and why incentives (don't) work to modify behavior. Journal of Economic Perspectives, 25, 191–209.

76. Gneezy, U., & Rustichini, A. (2000). A fine is a price. Journal of Legal Studies, 29, 1–18.

77. Mellström, C., & Johannesson, M. (2008). Crowding out in blood donation: Was Titmuss right? Journal of the European Economic Association, 6, 845–863.

78. Thaler, R. H., Sunstein, C. R., & Balz, J. P. (2012). Choice architecture. In E. Shafir (Ed.), The behavioral foundations of public policy (pp. 428–439). Princeton, NJ: Princeton University Press.

79. Brockington, D. (2003). A low information theory of ballot position effect. Political Behavior, 25, 1–27.

80. Hadar, L., Sood, S., & Fox, C. R. (2013). Subjective knowledge in consumer financial decisions. Journal of Marketing Research, 50, 303–316.

81. Hadar, L., Tannenbaum, T., & Fox, C. R. (2017). Subjective knowledge attenuates default effects. Working paper, Interdisciplinary Center Herzliya, Herzliya, Israel.

82. Tannenbaum, D., Fox, C. R., & Rogers, T. (2017). On the misplaced politics of behavioral policy interventions. Nature Human Behaviour, 1, Article 0130. https://doi.org/10.1038/s41562-017-0130

83. Forehand, M. R., & Grier, S. (2003). When is honesty the best policy? The effect of stated company intent on consumer skepticism. Journal of Consumer Psychology, 13, 349–356.

84. Costa, D. L., & Kahn, M. E. (2013). Energy conservation "nudges" and environmentalist ideology: Evidence from a randomized residential electricity field experiment. Journal of the European Economic Association, 11, 680–702.

85. Reisch, L. A., & Sunstein, C. R. (2016). Do Europeans like nudges? Judgment and Decision Making, 11, 310–325.

86. De Haan, T., & Linde, J. (2017). "Good nudge lullaby": Choice architecture and default bias reinforcement. The Economic Journal. Advance online publication. https://doi.org/10.1111/ecoj.12440

87. Goldstein, D. G., Johnson, E. J., Herrmann, A., & Heitmann, M. (2008). Nudge your customers toward better choices. Harvard Business Review, 86, 99–105.

88. Jones, E. E., & Davis, K. E. (1965). From acts to dispositions: The attribution process in person perception. In L. Berkowitz (Ed.), Advances in experimental social psychology (Vol. 2, pp. 219–266). Durham, NC: Duke University Press.

89. Chaiken, S., & Eagly, A. H. (1989). Heuristic and systematic information processing within and beyond the persuasion context. In J. S. Uleman & J. A. Bargh (Eds.), Unintended thought (pp. 212–252). New York, NY: Guilford Press.

90. Petty, R. E., & Cacioppo, J. T. (1986). The elaboration likelihood model of persuasion. In R. E. Petty (Ed.), Communication and persuasion (pp. 1–24). New York, NY: Springer.

91. Folkes, V. S. (1988). Recent attribution research in consumer behavior: A review and new directions. Journal of Consumer Research, 14, 548–565.

92. Pyszczynski, T. A., & Greenberg, J. (1981). Role of disconfirmed expectancies in the instigation of attributional processing. Journal of Personality and Social Psychology, 40, 31–38.

93. Weiner, B. (1985). An attributional theory of achievement motivation and emotion. Psychological Review, 92, 548–573.

94. Kahneman, D., & Miller, D. T. (1986). Norm theory: Comparing reality to its alternatives. Psychological Review, 93, 136–153.

95. Wood, W., & Quinn, J. M. (2003). Forewarned and forearmed? Two meta-analysis syntheses of forewarnings of influence appeals. Psychological Bulletin, 129, 119–138.

96. Campbell, M. C., Mohr, G., & Verlegh, P. W. J. (2012). Can disclosures lead consumers to resist covert persuasion? The important roles of disclosure timing and type of response. Journal of Consumer Psychology, 23, 483–495.

97. Bang, H. M., Shu, S. B., & Weber, E. U. (2018). The role of perceived effectiveness on the acceptability of choice architecture. Behavioural Public Policy. Advance online publication. https://doi.org/10.1017/bpp.2018.1

98. Felsen, G., Castelo, N., & Reiner, P. B. (2013). Decisional enhancement and autonomy: Public attitudes towards overt and covert nudges. Judgment and Decision Making, 8, 202–213.

99. Science and Technology Select Committee. (2011). Behaviour change (Second report of Session 2010–12, HL Paper 179). London, United Kingdom: House of Lords.

100. Steffel, M., Williams, E. F., & Pogacar, R. (2016). Ethically deployed defaults: Transparency and consumer protection through disclosure and preference articulation. Journal of Marketing Research, 53, 865–880.

101. Bruns, H., Kantorowicz-Reznichenko, E., Klement, K., Jonsson, M. L., & Rahali, B. (2018). Can nudges be transparent and yet effective? Journal of Economic Psychology, 65, 41–59. https://doi.org/10.1016/j.joep.2018.02.002

102. Kroese, F. M., Marchiori, D. R., & de Ridder, D. T. (2015). Nudging healthy food choices: A field experiment at the train station. Journal of Public Health, 38, e133–e137.

103. Loewenstein, G., Bryce, C., Hagmann, & Rajpal, S. (2015). Warning: You are about to be nudged. Behavioral Science & Policy, 1(1), 35–42.

104. Haynes, L., Service, O., Goldacre, B., & Torgerson, D. (2012). Test, learn, adapt: Developing public policy with randomized controlled trials. London, United Kingdom: Cabinet Office Behavioural Insights Team.

105. Giessen, P. (2018, February 4). Waarom dat getwijfel over de donorwet? Elders in Europa gaat orgaandonatie simpeler [Why the hesitation about the donor law? Elsewhere in Europe organ donation is done simpler]. Volkskrant. Retrieved from https://www.volkskrant.nl/wetenschap/waarom-dat-getwijfel-over-de-donorwet-elders-in-europa-gaat-orgaandonatie-simpeler~a4566096/

106. Nieuwe donorwet of niet, deze jonge mensen staan geen organen af [New donor law or not, these young people will not donate organs]. (2018, February 13). NOS. Retrieved from https://nos.nl/

op3/artikel/2216962-nieuwe-donorwet-
of-niet-deze-jonge-mensen-staan-
geen-organen-af.html

107. Rosdorf, M. (2018, February 14).
Vreugde en onrust op social media over
donorwet [Joy and unrest on social
media about donor law]. *EenVandaag*.
Retrieved from https://eenvandaag.
avrotros.nl/item/vreugde-en-onrust-
op-social-media-over-donorwet/

U.S. TREASURY

The role of choice architecture in promoting saving at tax time: Evidence from a large-scale field experiment

Michal Grinstein-Weiss, Cynthia Cryder, Mathieu R. Despard, Dana C. Perantie, Jane E. Oliphant, & Dan Ariely

abstract

Tax refunds give many low- and moderate-income (LMI) households a rare opportunity to save for unexpected expenses. We conducted three experiments aimed at increasing tax-time savings by LMI consumers. In a large field experiment, the most effective intervention increased the average savings deposits by about 50%. Delivered as people filed taxes online, this treatment consisted of a choice architecture intervention (a presentation of action choices that emphasized options for putting money into savings), combined with a message highlighting the need to save for emergencies. Two follow-up experiments simulated the tax-time situation and parsed components of the intervention. The first showed that the choice architecture and messaging interventions increased savings deposits independently. The second, assessing individual elements of the choice architecture intervention, showed that the mention of a savings option did not increase allocations by itself, but a heavy emphasis on savings or the ability to easily put money into savings did increase allocations.

Grinstein-Weiss, M., Cryder, C., Despard, M. R., Perantie, D. C., Oliphant, J. E., & Ariely, D. (2017). The role of choice architecture in promoting saving at tax time: Evidence from a large-scale field experiment. *Behavioral Science & Policy, 3*(2), 21–38.

A large fraction of American households live close to a financial cliff, lacking the savings to cover unforeseen expenses. Nationally representative data from the Pew Charitable Trusts[1] show that 41% of U.S. households do not have liquid savings to cover a $2,000 expense in an emergency; for low-income families, that rate increases to 78%.[2–4] Yet financial emergencies occur frequently: 60% of American households report experiencing a financial shock within the past year.[2] For consumers with low or moderate income (LMI), having savings can make the difference between meeting and failing to meet basic needs. When a job loss, a divorce, or some other crisis strikes,[5,6] savings can be tapped to cover such expenses as food, housing, and health care.[7,8] We define LMI households as having annual incomes below $35,000.

Tax refunds offer potential relief. A substantial percentage of LMI households are eligible for them,[9] and the refunds can constitute a sizeable portion of annual household income, often equaling an entire month of pay.[10] Tax refund time has, therefore, been identified as a "savable" moment for LMI consumers.[11] Indeed, it is the only time of the year when many can reasonably afford to divert money into savings.[12,13] Furthermore, households that deposit tax refunds into savings accounts have a reduced risk of material hardship—experiencing difficulty in meeting basic needs—in the six months following tax filing.[14]

For these reasons, policies that encourage LMI consumers to set aside some or all of their tax refunds into savings accounts could mitigate the risk of hardship.[15] Several such policies have been proposed, among them being the Refund to Rainy Day Savings Act of 2016[16,17] and the Financial Security Credit Act of 2015.[18] Reducing the risk of material hardship is an important policy goal given that difficulty in meeting basic needs too often goes hand in hand with child maltreatment,[19] impaired development,[20] parental mental health problems,[21] housing instability,[22] intimate partner violence,[23] and family stress.[24]

In the research described in this article, we assessed whether behavioral interventions that are low cost and low touch (easy to implement and receive) could increase tax-time savings by LMI consumers. Historically, interventions meant to increase savings by this group have not succeeded, perhaps because these individuals tend to have definite, preset plans for how to spend their refunds and such plans leave little leeway for efforts to influence their savings decisions.[25,26] Because devising interventions, or *treatments*, that increase savings for LMI consumers is so challenging, we tested a multi-pronged approach.

One element of our approach relies on increasing the salience of the savings deposit option via choice architecture. Broadly, *choice architecture* refers to any presentation of options; here, however, we define *choice architecture* as the presentation of options in a way that is meant to influence the choices made, typically without altering the actual options that are available.[27] Choice architecture has been shown to influence decisions as consequential as what energy-efficient car to drive,[28] how much money to allocate to retirement savings,[29] and whether to volunteer for organ donation.[30]

Increasing the salience of specific options—that is, increasing a decisionmaker's awareness of them—has also been shown to influence outcomes.[31] Previous research has identified salience as a primary driver of savings behavior.[32] For example, increasing the salience of saving by sending mail and text-message reminders can increase savings deposits.[33] In our research, we increased the salience of depositing tax refunds to savings accounts by using a choice architecture intervention that presented the savings deposit as an explicit option and put that option at the top of a list of available choices. (See the Appendices for the conditions and the screens the participants saw.)

A second element of our approach is *persuasive messaging*: communications crafted to change attitudes, opinions, or behaviors.[34,35] Persuasive messaging is ubiquitous in both commercial marketing and public policy campaigns and can influence behavior substantially.[36,37] Some previous attempts to use persuasive messaging to increase savings among LMI consumers have failed.[25] In the work described here, however, we heightened the urgency of the messaging, seeking to improve on those earlier attempts by, for example, explicitly describing the need for emergency savings rather than simply highlighting the necessity of a rainy day fund.[13]

Finally, the third element of our approach is increasing participants' involvement, or interaction, with savings messaging. Heightened involvement can influence responsiveness to persuasion attempts,[38] but only in some circumstances (such as when people are processing information carefully).[39] Here, we tested whether offering LMI consumers the opportunity to become more involved with persuasive messaging about savings increased the percentage who made savings deposits as well as the average amount of money deposited to savings accounts; specifically, we suggested various ways people might use their tax refunds and asked them to indicate the options that appealed to them most.

We report findings from three experiments. Experiment 1, with more than 600,000 participants, tested the combined effects of choice architecture, persuasive messaging, and involvement on real savings account deposits at tax refund time. On the basis of the results from Experiment 1, which suggested a positive influence of choice architecture and some forms of persuasive messaging, we designed Experiment 2. This experiment, with about 550 volunteers, was a simulation that isolated the choice architecture and persuasive messaging components from Experiment 1 to gauge the unique influence of each. Finally, on the basis of the collective results of Experiments 1 and 2—which both suggested that using choice architecture to heighten the salience of savings can be beneficial—we designed Experiment 3. This experiment, also with about 550 participants, was another simulation of the situation in Experiment 1; this time, we isolated individual components of the choice architecture intervention and determined which features were essential for increasing savings account deposits.

Experiment 1: Tax Refund Field Experiment

Experiment 1 was a large-scale field experiment that tested whether three different interventions that incorporated persuasive messaging, choice architecture, and involvement with messaging could increase the amount of refund money allocated by LMI consumers to savings accounts at tax time. The experiment was part of the Refund to Savings (R2S) Initiative, an ongoing collaboration between researchers at Washington University in St. Louis, Duke University, and Intuit, Inc. The experiment was embedded inside the TurboTax Freedom Edition (TTFE) tax preparation software offered free to qualified LMI tax filers as a part of the IRS Free File Program.[40] During the 2015 tax season, filers qualified for the TTFE if they had an adjusted gross income (AGI) of under $31,000, if they qualified for the Earned Income Tax Credit, or if a member of the household was on active military duty and the household had an AGI of under $60,000. The experiment ran from January 16 through June 7 of 2015. Intuit shared anonymous, aggregated tax data with the researchers in accordance with 26 U.S. Code § 7216.

Method

Participants. In the Method sections and appendices for each experiment discussed in this article and in the Supplemental Material, we report how we determined our sample sizes and any data exclusions and manipulations that were tested.[41]

See Table 1 for characteristics of the sample. The 646,116 participants were individuals who used TTFE and received a federal tax refund when filing in 2015. Their mean age was 35 years, and the mean AGI per household was $15,055, which is close to the 2015 poverty-line threshold for households with two members ($15,930);[42] the average number of dependents reported was 1.7. A greater percentage of Experiment 1 participants filed as single compared with all U.S. filers with income below the poverty line (67% versus 43%)[43] and compared with U.S. tax filers overall (47%).[40]

Compared with the general tax-filing population, Experiment 1 participants had lower

Table 1. Characteristics of participants in Experiment 1 (N = 646,116)

Characteristic	Value
Group assignment	
Control (*n*)	161,952
Choice Architecture + Emergency Savings Message (*n*)	161,011
Choice Architecture + Future Message + Involvement (*n*)	161,936
Choice Architecture + Retirement Message + Involvement (*n*)	161,217
Demographics	
Mean age[a] in years (*SD*)	35.25 (15.47)
Filing status	
Single	66.84%
Head of household	22.85%
Married, filing jointly, widow(er)	9.39%
Married, filing separately	0.92%
Any dependents	31.37%
Mean number of dependents, excluding none (*SD*)	1.71 (0.89)
Mean gross annual income[b] (*SD*)	$15,055 ($9,941)
Mean amount of federal tax refund (*SD*)	$2,030 ($2,379)
Active duty military	1.86%
Dividend income	5.77%
Unemployment benefits	5.97%
Interest income	12.71%
Retirement income	13.35%
Social Security benefits received	8.22%
Student loan tax credit	7.06%
Mortgage interest paid	6.34%
Real estate taxes paid (proxy for homeownership)	8.90%
American Opportunity Tax Credit (proxy for current students)	10.26%
Health insurance, full year	58.41%

Note. Means are weighted across groups. *SD* = standard deviation.

[a]Age is calculated on the basis of the difference between the weighted means of birth date at tax filing and filing date.

[b]Income is shown as the annual gross income for the household.

incomes; most (75%) had an annual income under $30,000, compared with 45% of all 2015 tax filers in the United States.[40] One third of Experiment 1 participants were younger than 25 years of age, compared with only 17% of all tax filers.

Procedure. Participants were randomly assigned to a control condition or one of three intervention conditions. (See Appendix A for screenshots of the choice architectures seen in all experimental conditions.) The TTFE software itself made the assignments after participants completed their federal income tax returns and learned they would receive a federal tax refund.

Participants randomly assigned to the control group received the standard TTFE screen, which prompted them to indicate how they wished to receive their refund. Control group participants had three options: (a) have the refund directly deposited into a bank account, (b) receive the refund via a paper check, or (c) split the money between multiple accounts. (This third option also included the ability to put the money into a U.S. Series I Savings Bond.) If participants chose to receive their refund via direct deposit, a subsequent screen prompted them to enter a bank account routing number, which could be for either a checking account or a savings account. The refund amount deposited to bank savings accounts serves as our operationalization of savings in this experiment and is our primary outcome of interest.

Participants in all three intervention groups viewed a savings-salient choice architecture screen showing four options. The two options at the top explicitly listed depositing refund money into a savings account—either all of it (listed first) or some of it (listed second). The third option was to directly deposit the entire refund into a checking or some other bank account, and the final option was to receive a paper check.

In addition, participants in the three intervention groups were randomly assigned to receive one of three messages: (a) a message highlighting the need for emergency savings,[44-46] (b) a message that mentioned saving for one's future and included an optional involvement component encouraging participants to interact with the messaging by selecting specific future financial goals, or (c) a message about retirement savings that also included an optional involvement component encouraging participants to select specific retirement savings goals (see the last three screenshots in Appendix A for the exact messaging). We labeled these interventions, respectively, Choice Architecture + Emergency Savings Message, Choice Architecture + Future Message + Involvement, and Choice Architecture + Retirement Message + Involvement.

We obtained our results through an intention-to-treat analysis,[47,48] meaning that we analyzed the effect of our manipulation on savings outcomes among all participants, whether or not they actually had savings accounts into which they could deposit tax refunds. The intention-to-treat approach is conservative and suggests that any observed effects are even stronger when looking only at individuals with savings accounts.

Results

Sample Balance. Sample balance was assessed across the four experimental groups to be sure that imbalances in participant characteristics did not confound the results. We evaluated balance for the following participant demographic characteristics: age, 2014 AGI, filing status, number of dependents, health insurance status, military status, and refund amount. In addition, we assessed sample balance with several additional variables that served as proxies for the financial characteristics and circumstances of participants. These included any income from the following sources: dividends or distributions, bank account interest, certain government payments (for example, unemployment benefits), retirement plan distributions, and Social Security benefits. Additionally, sample balance was assessed for child, student loan, and higher education expense–related (that is, American Opportunity and Lifetime Learning) tax credits; deductions for mortgage interest, real-estate tax, medical expenses, moving expenses, and health insurance expenditures for self-employed individuals; and tax filing date. We found no significant differences in any of these characteristics across our four groups. (We used aggregate data bivariate testing for covariates.) The lack of statistically significant differences across the four experimental groups indicates that randomization was effective and that the four groups did not differ in any systematic way on characteristics that might explain the differences in savings outcomes. In other words, differences in groups' savings outcomes may be attributed to the effects of the intervention, not to differences in the characteristics of participants.

Main Results. Table 2 shows the results from Experiment 1. As noted, the refund amount deposited to savings accounts served as our primary outcome of interest. Although a savings bond purchase was an option in all conditions, we excluded this form of savings because we were most interested in finding ways to increase the liquid financial assets accessible to LMI households for meeting household needs. Furthermore, the overall rate of savings bond purchases was extremely low (less than 0.1% in each condition); incorporating savings bond uptake into the outcome measure did not meaningfully influence the results.

Participants in each of the three intervention groups were significantly more likely to deposit some or all of their refunds into savings

41%

Households that do not have liquid savings to meet a $2,000 emergency expense

78%

Low-income households that do not have liquid savings to meet a $2,000 emergency expense

60%

Households that reported experiencing a financial shock in the previous year

Table 2. Effects of interventions in Experiment 1 (*N* = 646,116)

Condition	Amount deposited to savings account (*M*)	Deposited any of refund to savings account	Deposited entire refund to savings account
Control Choice Options + No Message	$160.25	8.44%	7.92%
Choice Architecture + Emergency Savings Message	$243.76***	13.34%***	12.54%***
Choice Architecture + Future Message + Involvement (the interactive future message)	$229.52***	12.60%***	11.83%***
Choice Architecture + Retirement Message + Involvement (the interactive retirement message)	$228.26***	12.40%***	11.63%***

Note. The *p* values were calculated in comparison to the control condition.
***p < .001

accounts than were participants in the control group. For example, 13.34% of participants who received the Choice Architecture + Emergency Savings Message intervention (hereinafter the *emergency savings message intervention*) allocated all or a portion of their refunds to a savings account, compared with 8.44% of control group participants, χ^2(1, *n* = 358,097) = 1,600, Cohen's *h* = 0.16, *p* < .001. (For more information about the statistics reported in this article, see note A.) In total, the treatment conditions led to an additional 20,916 tax filers depositing some or all of their refunds into savings accounts.

Within treatment groups, participants who received the emergency savings message intervention were significantly more likely to deposit refund money into savings accounts than were participants who received the Choice Architecture + Future Message + Involvement treatment (hereinafter called the *interactive future message intervention*), χ^2(1, *n* = 364,815) = 30.14, Cohen's *h* = 0.02, *p* < .001, or the Choice Architecture + Retirement Message + Involvement treatment (hereinafter called the *interactive retirement message intervention*), χ^2(1, *n* = 363,689) = 48.56, Cohen's *h* = 0.03, *p* < .001. A greater percentage of recipients of the interactive future message intervention put money into savings than did recipients of the interactive retirement message intervention, but the finding only approached statistical significance (*p* = .09).

Examining the average amount saved revealed similar patterns. Participants in each intervention group deposited significantly more money

into savings accounts than did participants in the control group. For example, participants who received the interactive retirement message intervention deposited an average of $68 more into savings accounts than control group participants did, *t*(315,104) = 20.74, Cohen's *d* = 0.07, *p* < .001. In total, the net increase in the refund saved due to treatments was $35,625,127, or an average of $73.59 per participant.

Some statistically significant differences in savings deposits were observed between treatment groups as well. On average, participants who received the emergency savings message intervention deposited $14 more to savings than did participants who received the interactive future message intervention, *t*(322,593) = 3.97, Cohen's *d* = 0.01, *p* < .001, and $16 more than did those who received the interactive retirement message intervention, *t*(321,896) = 4.33, Cohen's *d* = 0.02, *p* < .001. There was no statistically significant difference between the average savings deposits of filers shown the interactive future and interactive retirement messages, *t*(323,151) = 0.36, *p* = .72.

Subgroup Outcomes. The interventions also showed an impact when we stratified subjects by filing status and age. For each subgroup, we compared savings deposit rates and average deposits for the control group with those for the collected intervention groups (see Table 3). For example, participants who identified their tax filing status as single and received any one of the interventions deposited $43 more to savings than did their control group counterparts (*p* < .001), whereas intervention group participants who filed as head of household deposited $138 more to savings than did their control group counterparts ($p < .001$). One reason the 110,559 head of household filers in the intervention group deposited more on average than did the 323,679 single filers was because they received bigger refunds—an average of $4,796.15, compared with the single filers' average of $860.08.

Discussion

Experiment 1 demonstrated that choice architecture and messaging can substantially increase the percentage of LMI consumers who allocate tax refund money to savings accounts and can also increase the amount of money deposited. One particular intervention—choice architecture with an emergency savings message—appears somewhat more successful than the other treatments. It is possible that the heightened urgency of the emergency savings message played a role in this savings boost. The most notable effect, however, was that all versions of the treatment (choice architecture with some form of messaging) increased savings allocations compared with the control condition. Our experimental design did not allow for a direct assessment of whether having an involvement component in the messaging (selection of specific goals) affects savings decisions; we did not detect any clear benefit, however. In fact, the superiority of the emergency message intervention, which was not interactive, suggests that inviting involvement might have dampened the benefits of the other two treatments.

Although the intervention combining choice architecture with the emergency savings message performed better than all other treatments, the relative effects of choice architecture versus emergency messaging remained unclear. In Experiment 2, we isolated and compared the effects of the choice architecture and emergency savings messaging components through a simulated tax refund decision exercise.

Experiment 2: Choice Architecture Versus Messaging

In Experiment 2, we tested the choice architecture and emergency savings message interventions separately in an online tax refund decision simulation, gauging the unique

"Participants in each of the three intervention groups were significantly more likely to deposit some or all of their refunds into savings accounts"

Table 3. Treatment effects by subgroup in Experiment 1

Characteristic	Savings rate		Amount saved ($)	
	Control	Intervention	Control M (SD)	Intervention M (SD)
Filing status				
Single (n = 431,879)	8.26%	12.93%***	65.61 (338.85)	108.81*** (448.65)
Head of household (n = 147,646)	7.47%	9.88%***	390.84 (1,448.35)	529.08*** (1,670.77)
Age range (in years)				
15–24 (n = 211,605)	10.37%	15.24%***	81.19 (462.23)	119.13*** (543.55)
25–34 (n = 180,352)	6.52%	11.41%***	179.79 (930.89)	284.46*** (1,134.25)
35–44 (n = 90,747)	6.90%	9.67%***	286.36 (1,259.17)	402.80*** (1,481.16)
45–54 (n = 69,544)	6.99%	9.61%***	226.31 (1,055.81)	300.03*** (1,193.77)
55–64 (n = 57,833)	6.79%	9.83%***	153.80 (809.61)	214.53*** (931.48)
65+ (n = 36,035)	6.77%	9.78%***	89.99 (500.67)	132.99*** (622.13)

Note. SD = standard deviation.
***$p < .001$.

"Presenting the choice architecture manipulation alone or with the emergency savings message significantly increased the amount allocated to savings"

influence of each. We also tested whether the effects from Experiment 1 generalized to a new participant sample.

Method

Participants. Six hundred participants were recruited from Amazon Mechanical Turk and received $0.50 each for participating. We planned to have 150 participants in each of four conditions—sample sizes comparable to, yet still larger than, typical social science laboratory and survey experiments.[49] However, for both Experiments 2 and 3, which were conducted online via Amazon Mechanical Turk, we analyzed data only from those participants who passed an attention check test designed to weed out inattentive participants.[50,51] For Experiment 2, this procedure resulted in a total of 569 analyzed responses (median age = 34 years; 55% female, 45% male). Fifty-three percent of participants (n = 304) reported a tax filing status of single, and 33% (n = 188) reported a status of married, filing jointly. Seventy percent of participants reported having one or more savings accounts, and 97% reported having one or more checking accounts. Median annual household income within this sample fell in the range of $45,000 to $50,000; in the Results section, we report differences in patterns based on LMI (n = 207) versus non-LMI status (n = 360; two participants did not report household income).

Procedure. Participants were asked to imagine they had just filed their federal income tax returns and expected to receive a $1,000 refund (this approximates the median refund amounts in Experiment 1, which were $991 and $984 for treatment and control group participants, respectively). Participants were randomly assigned to one of four conditions (see Appendix B): (a) viewing only refund allocation options like those used in the control condition in the field experiment; (b) viewing refund options like those in the choice architecture condition in the field experiment, without any added messaging;

(c) viewing the control refund allocation options with an emergency savings message added; or (d) viewing the choice architecture with an emergency savings message added. This was a 2 (control, choice architecture) × 2 (no message, emergency savings message) between-subjects experimental design.

After participants made initial allocation decisions on the experimental screens, subsequent screens guided them through follow-up actions, including, for example, indicating exactly how much money to allocate to savings versus checking accounts. Here and in Experiment 3, the amount allocated to savings served as the operationalization of savings for the purposes of the experiment.

Results

Figure 1 shows the results. (See the Supplemental Material for more details.) Presenting the choice architecture manipulation alone or

Figure 1. Amount saved: Choice architecture & messaging interventions in Experiment 2

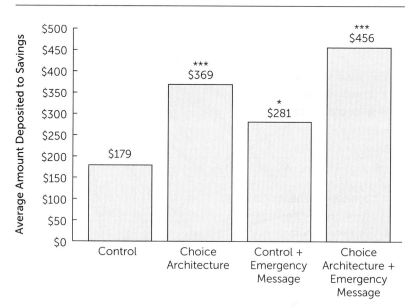

Note. The p values were calculated in comparison to the control condition, which did not contain an emergency message.
*p < .05.   ***p < .001.

Table 4. Savings outcomes based on choice architecture & messaging interventions in Experiment 2

Message	Amount deposited to savings account (M)	Deposited any of refund to savings account	Deposited entire refund to savings account
Control, no message	$178.57	18%	18%
Choice architecture, no message	$369.39***	41%***	31%*
Control + Emergency Savings Message	$280.64*	30%*	27%†
Choice Architecture + Emergency Savings Message	$456.07***	56%***	37%***

Note. The *p* values were calculated in comparison to the control condition.

†*p* < .10. **p* < .05. ****p* < .001.

with the emergency savings message significantly increased the amount allocated to savings compared with the amount allocated in the control condition, $F(1, 565) = 24.72$, $p < .001$. Adding the emergency savings message to either the control screen or the choice architecture screen also increased savings, $F(1, 565) = 6.57$, $p = .011$. The two treatments did not influence or interact with each other (that is, there was no statistically significant interaction between the two treatments). These results derive from a 2 × 2 analysis of variance. A different approach—a binary logistic regression—found a similar pattern. The patterns of statistical significance did not change when participants who failed the attention check were included in the analyses.

We also analyzed participants' responses on the basis of their income category. We found that the LMI consumers and non-LMI consumers responded in essentially the same way: they saved more when shown the choice architecture screen with no messaging, the control screen with the emergency savings message, or the choice architecture screen with the emergency savings message than they did when they viewed the control screen with no message. A different statistical analysis (a binary logistic regression) confirmed these patterns and suggested, albeit inconclusively, that the magnitude of the effects of choice architecture and of emergency messaging is similar for LMI and non-LMI individuals.

Discussion

In Experiment 2, we tested the choice architecture and the messaging manipulations separately, and each showed an independent effect on savings intentions; the combination of choice architecture and emergency messaging was more powerful than either manipulation alone because the effects were additive. Average savings were notably higher in this experiment than in the field experiment, probably because the participants were more affluent, on average, and were responding hypothetically. Nevertheless, the same manipulation that enhanced savings in the field experiment also increased savings intentions in a different population studied in a new context. In addition, the patterns held for both LMI and non-LMI participants, suggesting that these interventions may be effective across income groups.

Experiment 3: Effective Choice Architecture Components

In Experiment 3, we tested which elements of the choice architecture manipulation are essential to increasing deposits to savings accounts. We also once again tested whether any effects hold for both LMI and non-LMI participants.

Method

Participants. Six hundred participants were recruited from Amazon Mechanical Turk and received $0.50 for their participation. Following the procedures from Experiment 2, we analyzed data only from those participants who passed an exercise designed to identify and exclude inattentive participants, resulting in analyzed responses from a total of 554 participants (M age = 35 years; 56% female, 44% male). Of these, 54% (n = 300) reported a tax filing status of single, and 35% (n = 191) reported a status of married, filing jointly. Eighty percent of participants reported having one or more savings

Figure 2. Amount saved on the basis of choice architecture components in Experiment 3

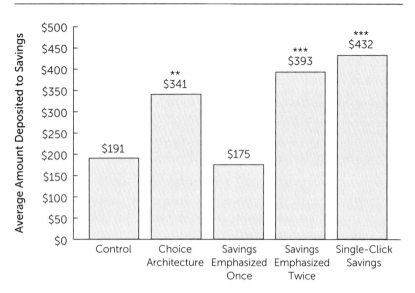

Note. The p values were calculated in comparison to the control condition
**p < .01.   ***p < .001.

accounts, and 98% reported having one or more checking accounts. Median annual household income in this sample fell in the range of $40,000–$45,000; in the Results section, we report differences in patterns based on LMI ($n = 221$) versus non-LMI ($n = 328$) status (five participants did not report household income).

Procedure. Participants were asked to imagine that they had just filed their federal income tax returns and expected to receive a $1,000 refund. Participants were randomly assigned to one of five experimental conditions that varied choice option descriptions. (See Appendix C.)

The first two conditions, control and choice architecture, replicated the control and choice architecture conditions from Experiment 2; neither included the messaging component. The three remaining conditions altered the choice architecture intervention slightly to evaluate which presentations of the savings option might be most effective. A *savings emphasized* condition listed a savings account option once; this option referred to putting "my entire refund or some of my refund" into a savings account. A *savings emphasized twice* condition included an option for depositing the entire refund into one or more savings accounts as well as an option for depositing some of the refund into savings. A *single-click savings* condition included a simple single-decision option that allowed participants to click once to allocate their entire refund to savings. After participants made the initial allocation decision on the experimental screens, subsequent screens guided them through detailed aspects of their choice (such as exactly how much money they wished to allocate to savings versus checking).

Results

Figure 2 and Table 5 display the results from Experiment 3, which replicate the pattern observed in results from Experiments 1 and 2: Participants in the choice architecture condition allocated significantly more money to savings accounts compared with counterparts in the control condition. (See Supplemental Material for more details.) Subjects in the choice architecture condition allocated an average of $340.68 to savings, whereas those in the control condition allocated an average of $190.91 to savings, $t(549) = 2.63$, Cohen's $d = 0.22$, $p = .009$.

Table 5. Savings outcomes based on choice architecture components in Experiment 3

Condition	Amount deposited to savings account (M)	Deposited any of refund to savings account	Deposited entire refund to savings account
Control	$190.91	19%	19%
Choice architecture	$340.68**	39%***	30%*
Savings emphasized	$174.76	21%	14%
Savings emphasized twice	$392.73***	44%***	35%**
Single-click savings	$431.86***	54%***	34%**

Note. The p values were calculated in comparison to the control condition.
*p < .05.   **p < .01.   ***p < .001.

Participants in the savings emphasized condition did not, however, allocate more to savings than did participants in the control condition ($174.76 and $190.91, respectively; $p > .25$), suggesting that merely emphasizing savings one time is not sufficient to influence refund allocations. A greater amount was allocated to savings by participants in both the savings emphasized twice condition ($M = \$392.73$), $t(549) = 3.45$, Cohen's $d = 0.29$, $p < .001$, and the single-click savings condition ($M = \$431.86$), $t(549) = 4.26$, Cohen's $d = 0.36$, $p < .001$, than by counterparts in the control condition. These patterns of significance did not change when participants who failed the attention check were included in analyses.

As in Experiment 1, we found that the savings allocation patterns held for both LMI and non-LMI consumers. We also again conducted further analyses, finding the results to be consistent with those reported above.

Discussion

In Experiment 3, we tested individual components of the choice architecture manipulation, demonstrating that heavily emphasizing saving and making saving a simple one-click decision both increased savings; however, simply including an explicit savings option among other options (the savings emphasized approach), even at the top of the list of choices, was not enough to increase savings deposits. The latter finding suggests that the increased savings seen in Experiments 1 and 2 were not achieved solely by reminding consumers that allocating money to a savings account is an option at tax time. Rather, it is important to put extra emphasis on deposits to savings, to increase the ease of making such deposits, or both. Once again, the observed effects held for both LMI and non-LMI participants, suggesting that choice architecture manipulations may be effective across income groups.

General Discussion

Although some previous researchers have struggled to find interventions that effectively increase savings deposits among consumers with low or moderate incomes,[25]

"it is important to put extra emphasis on deposits to savings, to increase the ease of making such deposits, or both"

in this article, we describe a choice architecture and messaging intervention that results in considerably higher savings by this financially vulnerable group. Further, this kind of intervention could feasibly be implemented on a large scale, because it is both low cost and low touch. Specifically, the use of a choice architecture and messaging that both emphasize savings could routinely be incorporated into online tax preparation software used by members of the IRS Free File Alliance to reach millions of LMI tax filers.

Experiment 1, a large-scale field experiment conducted with LMI consumers as part of the R2S Initiative, documents a choice architecture and messaging intervention (focused on saving for emergencies) that increased real deposits to savings accounts during tax refund time by approximately 50%. Experiment 2, a follow-up simulation experiment, separated the choice architecture and messaging manipulations, finding that each uniquely increased savings intentions. Experiment 3, another follow-up simulation experiment, tested individual features of the choice architecture intervention, finding that heavily emphasizing savings and making saving frictionless via the choice architecture each increased the intention to save; however, just mentioning savings once within choice options did not.

Although our primary focus in the research described in this article was developing interventions that increase savings deposits among LMI consumers, the results from Experiments 2 and 3 lead us to conclude that the intervention from Experiment 1—a choice architecture emphasizing savings combined with a message relating to the need to save for emergencies—is likely to increase savings for not only LMI consumers but other consumers as well. Our confidence that the approach described in this article can be effective is strengthened by previous findings. A similar project from tax year 2012 also showed that enhancing the salience of a savings option for tax refunds and providing messaging about the benefits can increase savings account deposits by LMI consumers.[13]

In that field experiment (N = 107,362), two manipulations that made savings salient were each tested alone and in combination with one of three accompanying messages. The two salience manipulations encouraged people to save either (a) 25% of the refund or (b) 75% of the refund. Two of the messages were motivational: one encouraged saving for retirement and one encouraged saving for a rainy day. The third message was a general one. The results for each of these eight conditions were compared with those from a control condition, consisting of the standard screen in TTFE software prompting tax filers to choose how they would like to receive their expected tax refund. All eight treatments increased savings account deposits relative to the deposits of participants in the control condition (overall treatment Cohen's h = 0.09), although the 75% allocation target with no additional messaging condition was slightly more effective than the others (Cohen's h = 0.13).[13] The current project—which increased savings salience via choice architecture and persuasive messaging—shows comparable although slightly larger effects (overall Cohen's h = 0.14; for the most successful treatment, the Choice Architecture + Emergency Savings Message, Cohen's h = 0.16).

Taken together, these projects suggest that altering the interface of tax-time filing software can increase savings account deposits among LMI consumers. The interventions most likely to succeed would include a choice architecture that makes savings salient together with motivational messaging that describes the need to put money into savings for emergencies.

Some may question whether one-time savings deposits are a meaningful measure of saving or even whether saving is the most beneficial use of tax refunds. Some recent research[52] has found that low-income tax filers often use refunds to reduce high-interest unsecured debt—an important financial priority that we do not capture in the current investigation. It may be better for low-income tax filers carrying high-interest-rate credit card debt to pay down some or all of this debt rather than to save, as the reduced interest costs will far exceed the paltry interest rate a conventional savings account will likely offer. Further, additional research finds that when consumers allocate money to savings, they may be unwilling to subsequently use those funds to cover nondiscretionary expenses[53] and may take on expensive debt to make ends meet.[54] Future research could track all of these outcomes, as well as survey measures of financial stress, to determine the optimal use of tax refund money for consumer well-being.

Nevertheless, tax-time refunds for LMI consumers do seem to provide a benefit, even though we cannot be certain that savings account deposits are the optimal use of the refunds. When consumers do not have emergency savings, they may be more likely to use high-cost financial services such as payday loans[55] to cope with emergency expenses and are at elevated risk for material hardship.[2,3] Further, previous research suggests that saving at tax time has benefits that persist: in a previous iteration of R2S, households that put money into savings vehicles at tax time were less likely to report material hardships six months after filing their taxes than were households that did not make savings deposits at tax time, and the result holds even after adjustments are made for observable differences between groups.[14] Options that enable people to deposit tax refunds into savings accounts easily when they file their tax forms may thus serve as "commitment mechanisms"[56]—ways for people to put money psychologically out of reach until it is truly needed.

Saved refunds can help people weather sudden losses of income or unanticipated expenses. We would like to see additional research explore the long-term financial and psychological health outcomes of interventions that increase tax-time savings deposits. The results of such work should help researchers develop interventions that yield the largest possible benefit to consumers' financial well-being.

endnote

A. Editors' note to nonscientists: For any given data set, the statistical test used—such as the chi-square (χ^2), the t test, or the F test—depends on the number of data points and the kinds of variables being considered, such as proportions or means. The p value of a statistical test is the probability of obtaining a result equal to or more extreme than would be observed merely by chance, assuming there are no true differences between the groups under study (the null hypothesis). Researchers traditionally view $p < .05$ as statistically significant, with lower values indicating a stronger basis for rejecting the null hypothesis. In addition to the chance question, researchers consider the size of the observed effects, using such measures as Cohen's d or Cohen's h. Cohen's d or h values of 0.2, 0.5, and 0.8 typically indicate small, medium, and large effect sizes, respectively.

author affiliation

Grinstein-Weiss, Cryder, Perantie, and Oliphant: Washington University in St. Louis. Despard: University of North Carolina at Chapel Hill. Ariely: Duke University. Corresponding author's e-mail: michalgw@wustl.edu.

author note

The Center for Social Development at Washington University in St. Louis gratefully acknowledges the funders who made the Refund to Savings Initiative possible: The Ford Foundation; the Annie E. Casey Foundation; Intuit, Inc.; the Intuit Financial Freedom Foundation; and JPMorgan Chase Foundation.

The Refund to Savings Initiative would not exist without the commitment of Intuit and its Tax and Financial Center, including the dedication of our collaborators: David Williams, Melissa Netram, Joe Lillie, Krista Holub, and many others on the Intuit team who have worked diligently in planning and implementing the experiment. Last, we thank the thousands of taxpayers who consented to participate in the research surveys and shared their personal financial information.

Disclaimer: Statistical compilations disclosed in this document relate directly to the bona fide research of and public policy discussions concerning savings behavior as it relates to tax compliance. Compilations are anonymous and do not disclose information containing data from fewer than 10 tax returns or reflect taxpayer-level data without the prior explicit consent from taxpayers. Compilations follow Intuit's protocols to help ensure the privacy and confidentiality of customer tax data.

supplemental material

- https://behavioralpolicy.org/publications/
- Additional Analysis

Appendix A. Screens viewed in Experiment 1

Control

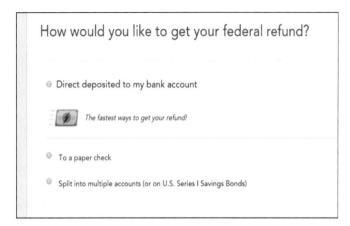

Choice Architecture + Retirement Message + Involvement

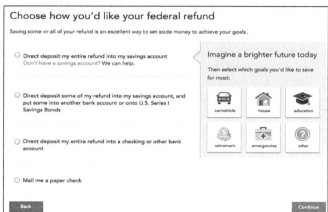

Choice Architecture + Emergency Savings Message

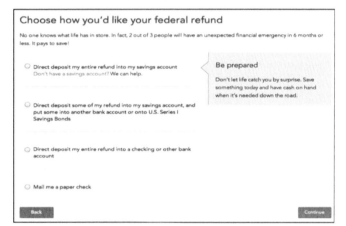

Choice Architecture + Future Message + Involvement

Note. The screenshots are from TurboTax Freedom Edition [Software], 2015, Mountain View, CA: Intuit. Copyright 2015 by Intuit. Reprinted with permission. All rights reserved.

Appendix B. The four conditions in Experiment 2

Control, No Message

Imagine that you just filed your federal taxes for the year and are eligible for a $1000 refund from the government.

How would you like to get your federal refund?

○ Direct deposit to my bank account
○ Mail me a paper check
○ Split into multiple accounts.

Control + Emergency Savings Message

Imagine that you just filed your federal taxes for the year and are eligible for a $1000 refund from the government.

No one knows what life has in store. In fact, 2 out of 3 people will have an unexpected financial emergency in 6 months or less. It pays to save!

BE PREPARED: Don't let life catch you by surprise. Save something today and have cash on hand when it's needed down the road.

How would you like to get your federal refund?

○ Direct deposit to my bank account
○ Mail me a paper check
○ Split into multiple accounts.

Choice Architecture, No Message

Imagine that you just filed your federal taxes for the year and are eligible for a $1000 refund from the government.

How would you like to get your federal refund?

○ Direct deposit my entire refund into a savings account
○ Direct deposit some of my refund into a savings account, and put some into another bank account
○ Direct deposit my entire refund into a checking account
○ Mail me a paper check

Choice Architecture + Emergency Savings Message

Imagine that you just filed your federal taxes for the year and are eligible for a $1000 refund from the government.

No one knows what life has in store. In fact, 2 out of 3 people will have an unexpected financial emergency in 6 months or less. It pays to save!

BE PREPARED: Don't let life catch you by surprise. Save something today and have cash on hand when it's needed down the road.

How would you like to get your federal refund?

○ Direct deposit my entire refund into a savings account
○ Direct deposit some of my refund into a savings account, and put some into another bank account
○ Direct deposit my entire refund into a checking account
○ Mail me a paper check

Appendix C. The five conditions in Experiment 3

CONTROL

How would you like to get your federal refund?

o Direct deposit to my bank account
o Mail me a paper check
o Split into multiple accounts

CHOICE ARCHITECTURE

How would you like to get your federal refund?

o Direct deposit my entire refund into a savings account
o Direct deposit some of my refund into a savings account, and put some into another bank account
o Direct deposit my entire refund into a checking account
o Mail me a paper check

Savings Emphasized Once

How would you like to get your federal refund?

o Direct deposit my entire refund or some of my refund into a savings account
o Direct deposit my entire refund into a checking account
o Mail me a paper check

Savings Emphasized Twice

How would you like to get your federal refund?

o Direct deposit my entire refund into one or more savings accounts
o Direct deposit some of my refund into a savings account, and put some into another bank account
o Direct deposit my entire refund into a checking account
o Mail me a paper check

Single-Click Savings

How would you like to get your federal refund?

o Direct deposit my entire refund into a savings account
o Direct deposit my entire refund or some of my refund into a checking account
o Mail me a paper check

references

1. Pew Charitable Trusts. (2015, November). *The role of emergency savings in family financial security: What resources do families have for financial emergencies?* [Issue brief]. Retrieved from http://www.pewtrusts.org/~/media/assets/2015/11/emergencysavingsreportnov2015.pdf

2. Pew Charitable Trusts. (2015, October). *The role of emergency savings in family financial security: How do families cope with financial shocks?* [Issue brief]. Retrieved from http://www.pewtrusts.org/~/media/assets/2015/10/emergency-savings-report-1_artfinal.pdf?la=en

3. Babiarz, P., & Robb, C. A. (2014). Financial literacy and emergency saving. *Journal of Family and Economic Issues, 35,* 40–50. http://dx.doi.org/10.1007/s10834-013-9369-9

4. Morduch, J., & Schneider, R. (2017). *The financial diaries: How American families cope in a world of uncertainty.* Princeton, NJ: Princeton University Press.

5. McKernan, S.-M., Ratcliffe, C., & Vinopal, K. (2009). *Do assets help families cope with adverse events?* (Perspectives on Low-Income Working Families Brief No. 10). Retrieved from Urban Institute website: http://www.urban.org/research/publication/do-assets-help-families-cope-adverse-events

6. Despard, M. R., Guo, S., Grinstein-Weiss, M., Russell, B., Oliphant, J., & De Ruyter, A. (in press). The mediating role of assets in explaining hardship risk among households experiencing financial shocks. *Social Work Research.*

7. Beverly, S. G. (2001). Material hardship in the United States: Evidence from the Survey of Income and Program Participation. *Social Work Research, 25,* 143–151. http://dx.doi.org/10.1093/swr/25.3.143

8. Gjertson, L. (2016). Emergency saving and household hardship. *Journal of Family and Economic Issues, 37,* 1–17. http://dx.doi.org/10.1007/s10834-014-9434-z

9. Internal Revenue Service. (2015). *Internal Revenue Service data book, 2014* (Publication No. 55B). Retrieved from https://www.irs.gov/pub/irs-soi/14databk.pdf

10. Internal Revenue Service. (2015). All returns: Number of returns, by age, marital status, and size of adjusted gross income, Tax Year 2013 (Table No. 1.6.). Retrieved from https://www.irs.gov/uac/soi-tax-stats-individual-statistical-tables-by-filing-status

11. Tufano, P., Schneider, D., & Beverly, S. (2005). *Leveraging tax refunds to encourage saving* (Retirement Security Project Paper No. 2005-8). Retrieved from https://www.brookings.edu/wp-content/uploads/2016/07/08_leveraging_tax_refunds.pdf

12. Barr, M. S. (2012). *No slack: The financial lives of low-income Americans.* Washington, DC: Brookings Institution Press.

13. Grinstein-Weiss, M., Russell, B. D., Gale, W. G., Key, C., & Ariely, D. (2017). Behavioral interventions to increase tax-time saving: Evidence from a national randomized trial. *Journal of Consumer Affairs, 51,* 3–26. http://dx.doi.org/10.1111/joca.12114

14. Grinstein-Weiss, M., Despard, M. R., Guo, S., Russell, B., Key, C., & Raghavan, R. (2016). Do tax-time savings deposits reduce hardship among low-income filers? A propensity score analysis. *Journal of the Society for Social Work and Research, 7,* 707–728. http://dx.doi.org/10.1086/689357

15. Black, R., & Schreur, E. (2014). *Connecting tax time to financial security: Designing public policy with evidence from the field.* Retrieved from New America Foundation website: https://www.newamerica.org/asset-building/connecting-tax-time-to-financial-security/

16. Halpern-Meekin, S., Greene, S. S., Levin, E., & Edin, K. (2018). The rainy day earned income tax credit: A reform to boost financial security by helping low-wage workers build emergency savings. *Russell Sage Foundation Journal of the Social Sciences, 4,* 161–176.

17. Refund to Rainy Day Savings Act of 2016, S. 2797, 114th Cong. (2016). Retrieved from https://www.congress.gov/114/bills/s2797/BILLS-114s2797is.pdf

18. Financial Security Credit Act of 2015, H.R. 4236, 114th Cong. (2015). Retrieved from https://www.congress.gov/bill/114th-congress/house-bill/4236

19. Kang, J. (2013). Instrumental social support, material hardship, personal control and neglectful parenting. *Children and Youth Services Review, 35,* 1366–1373. http://doi.org/10.1016/j.childyouth.2013.05.009

20. Gershoff, E. T., Aber, J. L., Raver, C. C., & Lennon, M. C. (2007). Income is not enough: Incorporating material hardship into models of income associations with parenting and child development. *Child Development, 78,* 70–95. http://dx.doi.org/10.1111/j.1467-8624.2007.00986.x

21. Heflin, C. M., & Iceland, J. (2009). Poverty, material hardship, and depression. *Social Science Quarterly, 90,* 1051–1071. http://dx.doi.org/10.1111/j.1540-6237.2009.00645.x

22. Desmond, M., & Kimbro, R. T. (2015). Eviction's fallout: Housing, hardship, and health. *Social Forces, 94,* 295–324. http://dx.doi.org/10.1093/sf/sov044

23. Ricks, J. L., Cochran, S. D., Arah, O. A., Williams, J. K., & Seeman, T. E. (2016). Food insecurity and intimate partner violence against women: Results from the California Women's Health Survey. *Public Health Nutrition, 19,* 914–923. http://dx.doi.org/10.1017/S1368980015001986

24. Cummings, E. M., & Davies, P. T. (1999). Depressed parents and family functioning: Interpersonal effects and children's functioning and development. In T. Joiner & J. C. Coyne (Eds.), *Advances in interpersonal approaches: The interactional nature of depression* (pp. 299–327). Washington, DC: American Psychological Association.

25. Bronchetti, E. T., Dee, T. S., Huffman, D. B., & Magenheim, E. (2011). *When a nudge isn't enough: Defaults and saving among low-income tax filers* (NBER Working Paper No. 16887). Retrieved from National Bureau of Economic Research website: https://www.nber.org/papers/w16887

26. Halpern-Meekin, S., Edin, K., Tach, L., & Sykes, J. (2015). *It's not like I'm poor: How working families make ends meet in a post-welfare world.* Berkeley: University of California Press.

27. Thaler, R. H., & Sunstein, C. R. (2008). *Nudge: Improving decisions about health, wealth, and happiness.* New Haven, CT: Yale University Press.

28. Larrick, R. P., & Soll, J. B. (2008, June 20). The MPG illusion. *Science, 320,* 1593–1594. http://dx.doi.org/10.1126/science.1154983

29. Thaler, R. H., & Benartzi, S. (2004). Save More Tomorrow: Using behavioral economics to increase employee saving. *Journal of Political Economy, 112*(Suppl. 1), S164–S187. http://dx.doi.org/10.1086/380085

30. Johnson, E. J., & Goldstein, D. (2003, November 21). Do defaults save lives? *Science, 302,* 1338–1339. http://dx.doi.org/10.1126/science.1091721

31. Taylor, S. E., & Thompson, S. C. (1982). Stalking the elusive "vividness" effect. *Psychological Review, 89,* 155–181. http://dx.doi.org/10.1037/0033-295X.89.2.155

32. Akerlof, G. A. (1991). Procrastination and obedience. *American Economic Review, 81*(2), 1–19.

33. Karlan, D., McConnell, M., Mullainathan, S., & Zinman, J. (2016). Getting to the top of mind: How reminders increase saving. *Management Science, 62,* 3393–3411. http://dx.doi.org/10.1287/mnsc.2015.2296

34. Chaiken, S. (1980). Heuristic versus systematic information processing and the use of source versus message cues in persuasion. *Journal of Personality and Social Psychology, 39,* 752–766. http://dx.doi.org/10.1037/0022-3514.39.5.752

35. Wood, W. (2000). Attitude change: Persuasion and social influence. *Annual Review of Psychology, 51,* 539–570. http://dx.doi.org/10.1146/annurev.psych.51.1.539

36. Banks, S. M., Salovey, P., Greener, S., Rothman, A. J., Moyer, A., Beauvais, J., & Epel, E. (1995). The effects of message framing on mammography utilization. *Health Psychology, 14,* 178–184. http://dx.doi.org/10.1037/0278-6133.14.2.178

37. Fishbein, M., Hall-Jamieson, K., Zimmer, E., Von Haeften, I., & Nabi, R. (2002). Avoiding the boomerang: Testing the relative effectiveness of antidrug public service announcements before a national campaign. *American Journal of Public Health, 92,* 238–245. http://dx.doi.org/10.2105/AJPH.92.2.238

38. Petty, R. E., Cacioppo, J. T., & Goldman, R. (1981). Personal involvement as a determinant of argument-based persuasion. *Journal of Personality and Social Psychology, 41,* 847–855. http://dx.doi.org/10.1037/0022-3514.41.5.847

39. Petty, R. E., Cacioppo, J. T., & Schumann, D. (1983). Central and peripheral routes to advertising effectiveness: The moderating role of involvement. *Journal of Consumer Research, 10,* 135–146. http://dx.doi.org/10.1086/208954

40. Internal Revenue Service. (2016). About the Free File Program. Retrieved from https://www.irs.gov/uac/about-the-free-file-program

41. Simmons, J. P., Nelson, L. D., & Simonsohn, U. (2012). *A 21 word solution.* Retrieved from: https://papers.ssrn.com/sol3/papers.cfm?abstract_id=2160588

42. U.S. Department of Health and Human Services. (2015). 2015 poverty guidelines for the 48 contiguous states and the District of Columbia [Table]. Retrieved from https://aspe.hhs.gov/2015-poverty-guidelines#threshholds

43. U.S. Census Bureau. (2015). *Current population survey: Annual social and economic supplement.* Retrieved July 20, 2016, from https://www.census.gov/did/www/saipe/data/model/info/cpsasec.html

44. Chase, S., Gjertson, L., & Collins, J. M. (2011). *Coming up with cash in a pinch: Emergency savings and its alternatives.* Retrieved July 20, 2016, from https://centerforfinancialsecurity.files.wordpress.com/2011/06/2011-coming-up-with-cash-in-a-pinch.pdf

45. Collins, J. M. (2015). Paying for the unexpected: Making the case for a new generation of strategies to boost emergency savings, affording contingencies, and liquid resources for low-income families. In J. M. Collins (Ed.), *A fragile balance: Emergency savings and liquid resources for low-income consumers* (pp. 1–15). New York, NY: Palgrave Macmillan.

46. Lusardi, A. (1998). On the importance of the precautionary saving motive. *American Economic Review, 88,* 449–453.

47. Hollis, S., & Campbell, F. (1999). What is meant by intention to treat analysis? Survey of published randomised controlled trials. *BMJ, 319,* 670–674. http://dx.doi.org/10.1136/bmj.319.7211.670

48. Newell, D. J. (1992). Intention-to-treat analysis: Implications for quantitative and qualitative research. *International Journal of Epidemiology, 21,* 837–841. http://dx.doi.org/10.1093/ije/21.5.837

49. Simmons, J. P., Nelson, L. D., & Simonsohn, U. (2013). Life after p-hacking. In *Proceedings of the Society for Personality and Social Psychology Fourteenth Annual Meeting* (pp. 17–19). New Orleans, LA: Society for Personality and Social Psychology.

50. Goodman, J. K., Cryder, C. E., & Cheema, A. (2013). Data collection in a flat world: The strengths and weaknesses of Mechanical Turk samples. *Journal of Behavioral Decision Making, 26,* 213–224. http://dx.doi.org/10.1002/bdm.1753

51. Oppenheimer, D. M., Meyvis, T., & Davidenko, N. (2009). Instructional manipulation checks: Detecting satisficing to increase statistical power. *Journal of Experimental Social Psychology, 45,* 867–872. http://dx.doi.org/10.1016/j.jesp.2009.03.009

52. Shaefer, H. L., Song, X., & Shanks, T. R. W. (2013). Do single mothers in the United States use the Earned Income Tax Credit to reduce unsecured debt? *Review of Economics of the Household, 11,* 659–680. http://dx.doi.org/10.1007/s11150-012-9144-y

53. Sussman, A. B., & O'Brien, R. L. (2016). Knowing when to spend: Unintended financial consequences of earmarking to encourage savings. *Journal of Marketing Research, 53,* 790–803. http://dx.doi.org/10.1509/jmr.14.0455

54. Gross, D. B., & Souleles, N. S. (2002). An empirical analysis of personal bankruptcy and delinquency. *The Review of Financial Studies, 15,* 319–347. http://dx.doi.org/10.1093/rfs/15.1.319

55. Collins, J. M., & Gjertson, L. (2013). Emergency savings for low-income consumers. *Focus, 30*(1), 12–17.

56. Benhabib, J., & Bisin, A. (2005). Modeling internal commitment mechanisms and self-control: A neuroeconomics approach to consumption–saving decisions. *Games and Economic Behavior, 52,* 460–492. http://dx.doi.org/10.1016/j.geb.2004.10.004

Phasing out a risky technology: An endgame problem in German nuclear power plants?

Markus Schöbel, Ralph Hertwig, & Jörg Rieskamp

abstract

Germany has twice decided to abandon nuclear energy. The first time, it set somewhat dynamic shutdown dates for plants before changing course. The second time, it set fixed shutdown dates. Game theory holds that awareness of shutdown dates may lead to *endgame behavior,* in which people at all levels of the industry behave more self-interestedly, thus potentially jeopardizing public safety, as the end dates approach. We examine whether such behavior is occurring in Germany by drawing on three sources of evidence: the public record, the frequencies of reportable safety-related events, and experimental data. The findings are inconclusive but suggest that the concerns merit consideration by policymakers in Germany or wherever policies need to be designed for the phaseout of dying industries. Counterintuitively, a policy designed to increase public safety may inadvertently create novel risks if it does not attend closely enough to the behavioral factors involved in its implementation.

Schöbel, M., Hertwig, R., & Rieskamp, J. (2017). Phasing out a risky technology: An endgame problem in German nuclear power plants? *Behavioral Science & Policy, 3*(2), 41–54.

Core Findings

What is the issue?
Decommissioning high reliability organizations such as nuclear power utilities carries risks of *endgame behavior*. With a finite horizon for operation, it is possible that agents will behave self-interestedly and shift behavior and investment away from safety. This, in turn, may increase the frequency of events with a higher safety significance as the shutdown date of a plant approaches.

How can you act?
Selected recommendations include:
1) Increasing data transparency in plant operations so that endgame risks can be assessed
2) Establishing innovative engineering programs focused on the decommissioning and dismantling of aging nuclear power plants

Who should take the lead?
Behavioral science researchers, and policymakers in energy.

n the wake of the Fukushima Daiichi nuclear accident in Japan in March 2011, the German government decided—once again—to phase out the country's use of nuclear energy. It was the second time the nation had opted to abandon nuclear energy. In 2001, the government had assigned each nuclear power plant a *residual electricity output*—a total amount of electricity it was to produce in the years ahead;[1] once that total was reached, the plant was to be taken off the grid. In October 2010, the government, now with different leadership in place, reversed this plan, deciding to allow the country's 17 nuclear plants to operate until at least 2036. But in June 2011, mindful of the public's concerns about nuclear safety after the Fukushima disaster and the recommendations of an expert commission, the government shut down eight plants immediately and specified shutdown dates for the remaining nine. These appointed dates ranged from 2015 to 2022 and cannot be exceeded. In other words, if anything disrupts energy production for a time (such as planned outages and unexpected events), the close date will not be extended to compensate for the hiatus.[2] This fresh commitment to closing down nuclear power plants was the start of Germany's *Energiewende*, or energy transition—its shift away from nuclear power and fossil fuels to renewable energies.

The 2011 phaseout policy was established to protect Germany from the risks of nuclear energy production in the long term. We argue that in the short term, the design of the phaseout scenario can have unintended consequences for nuclear safety. We base our argument in part on studies of game theory. Specifically, working in or managing a plant that is scheduled to be shut down on a specific date is not unlike participating in a repeated game that will end in the near future.[3-5] Empirical evidence from finitely repeated games predicts an increase in *endgame behavior*—a shift toward self-interested behavior as the game's conclusion draws near. In the case of Germany's nuclear power plants, this could mean that the industry or individual employees change their behavior as the shutdown date of each plant approaches, which could affect public safety.

Endgame Behavior in Finitely Repeated Games

Generally speaking, game theory considers conflict and cooperation between rational decisionmakers. Theorists analyze these interactions across a wide range of games, with different games representing different properties of real-world interactions. One important property is the time horizon: games can be one-shot or repeated. A repeated game with a finite time horizon is played a known, specific number of times. There are also indefinitely repeated games, in which the players do not know when the repetition will stop; that is, there is no preordained number of repetitions. In this article, though, we focus mainly on finite time horizons, because Germany's 2011 phaseout plan calls for reactors to be shut down on fixed dates.

Game theory holds that people who play finite games will behave the same way regardless of whether the game is played once or multiple times. In finitely repeated games, optimal behavior is determined by backward induction: players anticipate their optimal moves for the last period (that is, the last round) of the game, then for the second-to-last period, and continue the process backward to the first period. In theory, if a one-period game is repeated finitely, then the game-theoretical prediction for the one-period game holds for every period of the repeated game. For instance, in a *social dilemma* situation, in which a person can contribute to the general good or else behave opportunistically, game theory holds that a self-interested player should not contribute to a public good in either a one-period game or a finitely repeated game. Experimental economists have shown, however, that people do not strictly conform to this prediction. In fact, people initially cooperate in finitely repeated social dilemma games, but then endgame behavior takes over: cooperation typically declines and free riding increases over the course of the game.[5-9]

We suggest, therefore, that phaseout policies with predetermined shutdown dates carry the risk of fostering detrimental endgame behavior in any dying high-reliability organization—one that is prone to accidents unless great vigilance is maintained. In this context, we think of endgame behavior as a multilevel phenomenon, with safety risks stemming from self-interested behavior occurring at the level of the individual on up to the level of organizations.

To the best of our knowledge, no previous research has examined the potential risks of endgame behavior in high-reliability industries faced with organizational demise. At this point, the possibility that Germany's decision to phase out nuclear power is fostering endgame behavior can be analyzed only (a) conceptually (by drawing on the public record), (b) empirically (by analyzing the scant data available, that is, the frequency of reportable safety events), and (c) experimentally (by systematically manipulating the impact of simulated phaseout strategies on individual decisionmaking). In this article, we pursue all three routes.

Conceptual Observations: The Public Record

Which conditions may undermine nuclear safety? These days, experts in industrial safety favor a systems approach to managing risks in high-reliability organizations.[10–12] They model the critical components of risk management across a hierarchy of levels—from legislation to government agencies, industry associations, utility and plant management, and single-plant employees. People and organizations at higher levels impose constraints on the activities of the people and organizations at subordinate levels. Endgame behavior, manifested as a shift toward self-interested behavior,[6] may occur at any of these levels and wherever the levels interact.

At the top levels, an impending shutdown may change the interactions between utility companies and government agencies, reducing the companies' incentives to meet regulatory demands. The public record catalogs several key events that may be interpreted as signs of deterioration in the trust and collaborative relationships between companies and the government.

For instance, after a few years in which profits from nuclear and fossil fuel power generation slumped,[13] in 2014, the utilities proposed that ownership of all nuclear power plants and the associated risks should be transferred to a public trust. The trust would be responsible for operating the plants until they wound down and then for their decommissioning and dismantling, as well as for the final disposal of radioactive waste. In other words, the trust would free the utilities from any liability. In exchange, the utilities would contribute around €30 billion in reserves that they had been required to build up over time to cover the costs of dismantling plants and managing nuclear waste.[14] In 2016, a federal government commission set up to review the financing of the nuclear phaseout issued a final report rejecting this proposal and instead recommending a division of labor: companies would retain the responsibility and unlimited liability for operating, decommissioning, and dismantling plants and packing radioactive waste, whereas the government would take responsibility for the waste's intermediate storage and for the operation of the final repositories.[15] In late June 2017, Germany's economy ministry and the country's four utility companies formally agreed to that proposal, and in July 2017 the companies paid €24.1 billion into the newly created "Fund for Nuclear Waste Management."

In another sign of stress between the utilities and the government, in 2014, Germany's biggest utility company, E.ON, announced plans to split into two companies, one focusing on nuclear and fossil fuel and the other on renewable energies. According to media reports, "many observers took E.ON's decision to hive off the fossil-fuel and nuclear-generation business as the creation of a kind of 'bad utility'—like the 'bad banks' created to house toxic assets after the financial crisis."[16] However, once the German government proposed making companies permanently liable for the costs of dismantling reactors, E.ON canceled its plans to spin off its German (although not its Swedish) nuclear power plants.

Furthermore, the German utilities E.ON and RWE and the Swedish utility Vattenfall sued the German government over the legality of the 2011 nuclear phaseout. The case reached the Federal Constitutional Court (Germany's

"endgame behavior could be manifested as decreasing efforts by industry to maintain the skills and motivation of its workforce"

highest court) in 2016, with the utilities accusing the German state of expropriating their atomic plants without paying compensation.[17] In December 2016, the court mostly rejected their claims, deeming the law for a nuclear phaseout "mostly compatible with Germany's constitution."[18] In another lawsuit, though, the court ruled in June 2017 that a nuclear fuel tax imposed on energy utilities in 2011 was unconstitutional, which, in turn, allowed nuclear utilities to claim billions of euros in refunded taxes. Relatedly, Vattenfall has filed a request for arbitration against Germany at the International Centre for Settlement of Investment Disputes. According to Germany's Federal Ministry for Economic Affairs and Energy, Vattenfall is asking for €4.7 billion ($6 billion) in compensation for the nuclear shutdown.[19]

Aside from what media observers describe as a "bruising confrontation"[17] between utilities and the German government in the courts, endgame behavior could be manifested as decreasing efforts by industry to maintain the skills and motivation of its workforce and, by extension, the level of nuclear safety. As early as 2012, the German Reactor Safety Commission (RSK), which gives nuclear safety advice to the Federal Ministry for the Environment, Nature Conservation and Nuclear Safety, published a memorandum warning of the loss of know-how and motivation among plant employees.[20] Specifically, the commission exhorted management not to give the workforce the impression that it is viewed as a somewhat difficult and marginalized group and to offer employees ways to continue their careers. At the end of 2016, the RSK reiterated its concerns from the 2012 memorandum.[21] After consulting representatives of contractor organizations,

agencies, regulators, and utility companies from the German nuclear industry, the RSK recommended that these entities should implement change-management measures (such as monitoring, evaluating, and supporting processes of change) and establish procedures for documenting and monitoring the competencies of all employees.

The RSK recommendations were made in response to past developments in the German energy supply market and to concerns about the future effects of the phaseout decision on the plants that are still operating. All utilities have implemented far-reaching cost-cutting measures in response to the 2011 phaseout decision. For instance, Areva, one of the largest on-site contractors in the German nuclear power industry, with several thousand employees, has reduced staff due to a site closure.[22] For its part, RWE attempted to negotiate with the union to get a 25% wage cut for all employees in the power generation division,[23] and E.ON's nuclear unit has recently announced that it will cut at least half of its workforce by 2026.[24]

The utilities' publicly available financial reports do not detail exactly where costs have been cut. Therefore, the extent to which utilities continue to invest in technical system upgrades, continuous training, safety culture initiatives, and on-site contractors is unknown. It is unlikely, however, that new investments in complex technical safety upgrades, which can take years to implement, are in the works. By the terms of the 2011 nuclear power phaseout plan, the plant outages that would be required to enable the installation of safety upgrades would reduce plants' remaining operation times, which would make safety investments increasingly difficult to justify on purely economic grounds.[25] Even if investments are still made and jobs are not cut, a relative decline in expertise will be inevitable, because the industry is losing its ability to attract highly qualified new workers. Indeed, German universities have a dearth of new students in nuclear safety engineering, even though such knowledge will be needed to operate the intermediate and final repositories. Relatedly, reports indicate that the industry has reduced or ended its support for nuclear engineering research at universities.[26]

These signs of the utilities' disengagement—along with the extensive media coverage of the industry's financial difficulties and pending demise—have no doubt affected plant employees. Although no data are publicly available, it seems reasonable to suspect that a brain drain—the emigration of highly marketable employees—is leaving behind a negatively selected group to oversee the plant's final operation and transition to retirement. Research suggests that job insecurity, as is faced by this group, is associated with declining safety knowledge and dwindling motivation to comply with safety policies, which may, in turn, lead to more accidents and to injuries in the workplace.[27]

Even though the situation in Germany seems to make the unraveling of safety standards and behaviors more likely than before, a strong organizational safety climate could potentially attenuate the threat.[28] Yet even relatively subtle psychological responses to pending organizational demise can pose a risk. According to a thesis known as the *threat-rigidity hypothesis,* individuals and groups tend to behave rigidly in dying organizations.[29] Rigid behavior—in terms of less mindful information processing, less vigilance and attention, unwillingness to take responsibility and to learn, and work-to-rule activity—can undermine important safety behaviors (such as mindful and questioning behavior),[30,31] especially if the organization has a weak safety climate.

Frequencies of Reportable Events

Beyond the trends described above, are there quantifiable empirical indications of an endgame dynamic in the German nuclear power industry? Such indicators as near-miss reports or management audits of single plants are not publicly available and therefore cannot be investigated. We can, however, examine one important and publicly available indicator of nuclear plant safety: the frequency of reportable events. In Germany, the Nuclear Safety Officer and Reporting Ordinance obliges nuclear

power facilities to report all events of "higher safety significance"—such as malfunctions, unexpected outages, and incidents known as *process safety accidents*—to the Incident Registration Centre of the Federal Office for the Safety of Nuclear Waste Management.[32]

The endgame hypothesis suggests that the frequency of reportable events in German nuclear power plants will increase as the shutdown date of a plant approaches. Several factors complicate the analysis of whether this suggestion is correct, however. First, there is no firm theoretical ground for predicting the precise moment at which the endgame starts (that is, the onset of a potential endgame). Second, different players within the same company may experience and perceive the terminal stages of a dying industry differently. For instance, the management of a utility is accountable for all of its plants, and this responsibility extends beyond the closure of a single plant. In contrast, the employees of that plant are immediately affected by the utility's restructuring plans.

Notwithstanding these difficulties, one way to probe potential endgame effects in German nuclear power plants is by contrasting the annual frequencies of reportable events before and after the 2011 phaseout decision. To this end, we determined the average frequency of events occurring five years before and five years after the 2011 decision at the eight plants then still operating (using the annual reports from 2006 to 2016 of the Incident Registration Centre of the Federal Office for the Safety of Nuclear Waste Management). Contrary to the endgame hypothesis, the average frequencies of reportable events for these plants were relatively stable within the five-year period before and after the 2011 decision: the half-year means were 2.40 and 2.35, respectively (see Figure 1A; see also the frequencies of reportable events listed separately for individual plants in the Supplemental Material).

We wondered whether the pattern was similar after the 2001 shutdown decision. In that case, Chancellor Schröder and representatives of the German nuclear industry signed an agreement to phase out nuclear energy over the next 20

€24.1 billion
Contribution cost to German energy utilities for a state fund to store nuclear waste and operate final repositories

39%

Increase in average frequency of reportable events at Germany's nuclear plants after the 2001 shutdown decision

234
Number of operating nuclear reactors worldwide that are more than 30 years old

years (in what become known as the *nuclear consensus*). The agreement became law in April 2002. Recall that, in contrast to the 2011 phaseout decision, the shutdown dates were not fixed; plants would be taken off the grid when their assigned residual electricity output was reached. The termination dates could vary because output allowances could be transferred from one plant to another and because unplanned and planned outages (such as for maintenance work or the technical upgrading of plants) would delay the final shutdowns. It was nonetheless clear that as they approached the allotted electricity output, the shutdown day came closer and the probability of termination increased. When the probability of termination increases over time, game theory predicts endgame behavior. Although no one knows exactly when the termination probability will cross a critical threshold—after which, for instance, safety investments are no longer paying out—it is likely that at some point, this threshold will be reached; therefore, endgame behavior should be expected.

As in the first analysis, we examined the average frequencies of reportable events during five-year windows before and after the 2001 decision (using the annual reports from 1996 to 2006 obtained from the Incident Registration Centre of the Federal Office for the Safety of Nuclear Waste Management). Figure 1B shows that during the five years directly after the 2001 decision, the average half-year frequency of reportable events of the 17 operational plants increased by 39%, from 2.79 to 3.87 events (in an exact two-tailed Wilcoxon signed rank test, $W = 16.5$, $p = .003$). (See note A.) Specifically, the number of events increased in 15 of the 17 plants.

In other words, we found an increase in the annual frequency of reportable events in the wake of the 2001 but not the 2011 phaseout decision. We do not have a clear explanation for the difference, but we can see a number of possible contributing factors. One is that the politics surrounding the 2001 situation makes it hard to know when the endgame is most likely to have commenced. Perhaps we looked at the wrong time interval. As mentioned earlier, there

is, in any case, no firm theoretical ground for predicting the timing of the onset of endgame behavior. Also, although the nuclear power legislation did not become law until 2002, the end of nuclear energy generation in Germany was already predictable at the time of the 1998 elections, which saw victories by the Green Party and the Social Democrats. The agreement between the German government and the energy companies was reached in 2000 and endorsed by both parties in 2001. This more prolonged decision time line, combined with the different phaseout architectures of the 2001 and 2011 plans, also means that one cannot draw any firm conclusions from the 2001 case about when endgame behavior, as manifested by higher frequencies of reportable events, is likely to start in the nuclear power plants that are operating in Germany today.

We can envision a couple of additional reasons for the different outcomes. The two phaseout decisions were caused by incommensurable events: the Greens and Social Democrats winning the German federal election versus the Fukushima Daiichi nuclear disaster. The nuclear disaster, unlike the election victory, may have caused the nuclear power industry and its employees to be on full alert, even more than usual. Also, the phaseout decisions could have differed in their influence on the plants' reporting thresholds. Plant managers have some freedom in deciding whether and when an event is reported, and utilities may exploit this wiggle room to different extents. Because the 2001 decision allowed plants to extend their operating time if they had production outages, the plants may have been more willing to report events and take the time needed to address them. But for today's plants, any production outages (such as those for events that require technical upgrading to fix or a prolonged and deepened root-cause analysis) and associated financial losses cannot be recouped in the future. This constraint may result in a higher threshold for what constitutes a reportable event. Admittedly, all these explanations are speculative.

Can the different outcomes be better understood by considering what is happening in

Figure 1. Average frequencies of reportable events (per half year) five years before & after (A) the 2011 phaseout decision (for the eight operating plants) & (B) the 2001 phaseout decision (for the 17 operating plants)

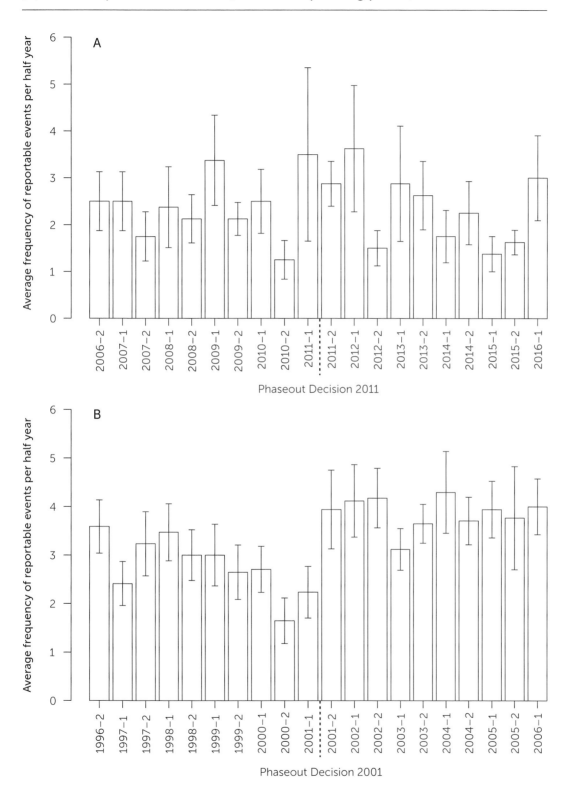

Note. Reportable events meet the German Nuclear Safety Officer and Reporting Ordinance criteria for higher safety significance, such as malfunctions, unexpected outages, or process safety incidents (Federal Office for the Safety of Nuclear Waste Management, 2016). Error bars represent an interval of ±1 standard error of the mean, the extent of deviation from the mean.

a publication of the behavioral science & policy association   47

"there is reason to worry that phaseout decisions in a dying high-reliability industry could carry an increased risk of detrimental endgame effects"

other countries? Germany, after all, is not the only country in which nuclear power is being phased out. Our study of nuclear phaseout policies in other countries, however, has identified only one case that seems comparable with the German situation, involving a substantial delay between a political decision and the actual industrial shutdown: Sweden. In 1997, long after a 1980 referendum in which the majority of the Swedish population voted to phase out nuclear power, the government passed phaseout legislation.[33] On the basis of this phaseout act, the Swedish government decided that the Barsebäck 1 reactor would be closed in June 1998, and the Barsebäck 2 reactor would be shut down in July 2001. After the Swedish supreme administrative court rejected an appeal against the decision submitted by the plant's owner in June 1999, Barsebäck 1 was permanently shut down in November 1999. Barsebäck 2, in contrast, was not shut down until May 2005, after repeated postponements of the shutdown date due to a lack of renewable energy to replace its output.[34] It is interesting that in 2004, shortly before its closure, Barsebäck 2 reached an all-time peak in production. At the same time, reportable events at Barsebäck 2 increased from 21 in 2002 to 48 in 2004 (see Figure S3 in the Supplemental Material). Final bursts of productivity have also been reported for conventional organizations facing terminal shutdown.[35] The increase of reportable events may be consistent with the extended endgame period of Barsebäck 2, at the expense of a usually strong emphasis on safety. This single case, however, defies any general conclusions.

To conclude, the data on reportable events before and after Germany's phaseout decisions paint a mixed picture. Nevertheless, the findings for the operational plants after the 2001 decision and for the operational Swedish Barsebäck 2 reactor suggest that there is reason to worry that phaseout decisions in a dying high-reliability industry could carry an increased risk of detrimental endgame effects. We emphasize that the case is not yet strong, however, and that the specifics of the situations could be important. Some plants contributed more to the increase in reportable events than others, for instance (see the Supplemental Material). Moreover, the data we examined are not free of noise and bias. For instance, the date of reporting can deviate from the date of the event, and single plants may have varying reporting thresholds.[36]

Experimental Evidence of Endgame Effects on Safety-Relevant Investments

Experimental results have successfully informed a wide range of public policy and institutional design decisions, such as auctions for electric power in California[37] and the British 3G telecom licenses auction.[38] Against this background, we investigated the potential impact of endgame effects on safety in controlled experimental studies simulating two phaseout strategies. One strategy simulated a fixed shutdown date (*finite horizon condition*), which parallels the 2011 and, to some extent, also the more dynamic 2001 phaseout scenarios. The other simulated a constant probability of further operations (*indefinite horizon condition*). (See the Supplemental Material for more details on the method, hypotheses, and results.) In games with an indefinite time horizon, after each game period another period follows with some probability so that the players do not know how many times the games will repeat. In this context, unlike the situation in finitely repeated games, behavior based on rational self-interest can now coincide with socially desired behavior. As long as there is a substantial probability of future interaction and the probability of termination is low, people are predicted to refrain from exploiting others, and cooperation (or contribution to a public good) can be sustained. Our goal in Study 1 was to examine whether behavior in a scenario involving safety depends on endgame horizons.

A total of 62 participants acted as managers of a hypothetical chemical plant. Operation of the plant could result—with a probability of 5%—in a very costly accident. To avoid this accident, managers could invest in safety measures that kept the accident probability constant but carried costs. Alternatively, they could decide against investing in safety, thus incurring no costs, but the probability of an accident increased.

To examine the impact of a finite compared with an indefinite time horizon, we had half the managers make decisions knowing that the plant would be closed in 10 experimental years. For the other half, no definite closing time was specified. The game-theoretical predictions for the two time horizons are clear: In the finite horizon condition, there is a conflict between payoff maximization and safety investment; optimal payoff-maximizing behavior involves no investments after the third period of the game. In the indefinite horizon condition, safety investments are always the optimal and payoff-maximizing decision. (For additional details, see the Supplemental Material.)

The rationale behind these predictions is relatively simple: Investments in safety keep the probability of future accidents low, but when the future is limited—as in the finite horizon condition—keeping the probability of an accident low does not pay off. In contrast, because of the uncertainty about the length of the game in the indefinite horizon condition, the expected value of safety investments is always positive, making safety investment the payoff-maximizing choice. In both conditions, managers' investment choices largely followed the expected logic. As shown in Figure 2A, in the finite horizon condition, safety investments—as measured by the proportion of decisions intended to increase safety compared to all decisions—declined markedly as the shutdown of the plant approached. In the indefinite horizon condition, in contrast, the investments increased from the first to the sixth periods (56% versus 71%) and then remained constant.

We tested the robustness of Study 1's findings in a second study. In Study 2, we implemented

Figure 2. Proportion of yearly investments targeted to safety in (A) Study 1 & (B) Study 2

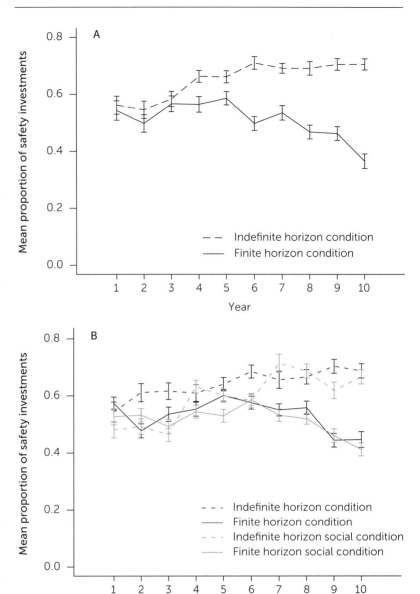

Note. The mean proportion of safety investments is the average number of investment choices intended to increase safety when compared with all decisions. Smaller proportions signify lower commitments to safety. Error bars represent an interval of ±1 standard error of the mean.

the same experimental paradigm and horizon manipulation but in addition tested whether imposing collective consequences for choosing not to invest in safety would alter behavior. Omitting safety investments not only affects people's own outcomes but can also have negative consequences for other people. We reasoned, therefore, that people with other-regarding social preferences might be motivated to choose the safety investment to avoid negative consequences for others.

In Study 2, a total of 427 participants were assigned to one of four experimental conditions. There were two social groups and two nonsocial groups, each with a finite or an indefinite horizon. We analyzed the behavior of only the 115 participants who demonstrated an understanding of the game by passing a knowledge test about it and who had not participated in more than 20 online surveys in the past month. Participants in the two social groups were informed that they would be randomly and anonymously grouped with three other participants in the experiment. If any member of that group was responsible for an accident's occurrence, the other three group members would also incur costs.

As Figure 2B shows, the findings of Study 1 were replicated, with declining proportions of safety investments in the finite but not the indefinite horizon condition. We had expected that participants in the social conditions would choose the safety investment option more often than would those in the corresponding nonsocial conditions, but we were wrong. The safety investment results did not differ substantially between the social and nonsocial conditions, and collective consequences did not prevent the observed endgame effect in the finite horizon condition.

In both studies, participants did not strictly follow the predictions of game theory: Those in the finite horizon condition did not completely stop investing in safety, and participants in the indefinite horizon condition did not always invest in safety. Nevertheless, the combined results demonstrate that a finite horizon triggered a declining investment in safety. An indefinite horizon, in contrast, resulted in a constant level of investments. Following the convention of experimental economics, players' outcomes depended on the other players' behavior in the social condition of the game, thus constituting a social interaction. It is, of course, conceivable that with additional face-to-face communication among players, the behavior could have turned out differently and might have led to more decisions to invest in safety than we saw.

Discussion & Conclusion

Our goal was to conceptually, empirically, and experimentally explore the possibility that the phaseout policies of the German government are having unintended consequences for the safety of the country's nuclear power industry. Phaseout policies in Germany were put in place to increase public safety and, in the case of the 2011 decision, to respond to the shift in public risk perception after Fukushima.[39,40]

Our analyses highlight in different ways the potential risk of endgame behavior during the phaseout window of a dying industry. First, drawing on the public record, we chronicled the increasingly adversarial dynamics between the state and industry players tasked with maintaining high levels of safety in German nuclear power plants. Second, the analysis of reportable events after two phaseout decisions revealed mixed evidence for endgame behavior on the plant level. On the one hand, we found no increase of reportable events during the five years after the 2011 decision compared with the five years before. On the other hand, we found significantly higher average frequencies of reportable events during the five years after the 2001 decision than during the five years before the decision. Additionally, we found an increase in reportable events at the Barsebäck 2 reactor in Sweden shortly before its final shutdown. Third, the results of our two experimental studies show that endgame behavior occurs at the level of individual players in a finite-horizon scenario, even in scenarios where low safety investments can lead to negative consequences for other players.

Let us clearly emphasize that we have found mixed results and could not help but rely on small sample sizes for the plants' reportable events. Therefore, our conclusions are neither clear-cut nor very strong. Moreover, we were not able to reveal the reasons for the inconsistent findings. We tried repeatedly, persistently, and through various channels—but ultimately unsuccessfully—to get additional data about the plants, such as reports of near misses related to safety, data on personnel turnover, and statistics on occupational accidents or sick leave of plant personnel. In line with the abovementioned recommendations of the RSK, we advocate for more transparency about these and other figures that could help to indicate whether managers and employees of nuclear power plants are slipping into endgame behavior.

In light of the potentially disastrous consequences of declining safety in nuclear power plants, we believe that our analysis of the respective phaseout policies is important enough to warrant attention from policymakers, utilities, and the public. Even if the empirical evidence we provide is limited and mixed, the theoretical argument that endgame effects should be taken into account when creating phaseout policies appears important. For example, according to the German Atomic Energy Act (section 19a, paragraph 2), a plant is required to undergo a comprehensive safety review every 10 years, unless the plant is to be taken off the grid within the three years that follow what would be the next scheduled review.[41] This means, for instance, that for the three plants that are scheduled to be shut down in 2022, the final comprehensive safety review occurred in 2009. One may question whether the waiver of an encompassing safety review is a wise decision in view of the potential endgame problems we have outlined; perhaps some version of the review should still be done. We, of course, hope that our concerns prove to be overly pessimistic. Nevertheless, we feel that an awareness of the risks embodied by endgame problems should intensify all stakeholders' efforts to prevent such an outcome—not only in Germany but also in other countries (such as Belgium and Switzerland) that have announced plans to phase out nuclear power.

The risks of endgame behavior deserve policymakers' attention because numerous factors may collude to amplify its potential impact. First, endgame behavior manifested as a shift toward self-interested behavior can occur across a hierarchy of levels, affecting the decisions of industry and policymakers, managers, and employees. The manifestation of endgame behavior is thus likely to be multidimensional—from employees showing increasingly rigid behavior, to the media vilifying employees of a dying industry (a risk highlighted by the RSK),[21]

"endgame behavior manifested as a shift toward self-interested behavior can occur across a hierarchy of levels"

to the industry trying to absolve itself from any midterm or long-term liability for plants and radioactive waste. These dynamics are intensified by developments that are likely in a phaseout period even without endgame behavior, such as difficulties in recruiting new talent and retaining skilled staff at all levels (operators, regulators, technical support workers, and suppliers).

What are the possible responses to these risks? One strategy to reduce the risk of noncooperative endgame behavior related to safety would be to not give employees advance notification of a plant's shutdown.[42] The results of the experimental studies suggest that endgame behavior is less likely to occur when the game has an indefinite time horizon. As long as the shutdown date is not known and unlikely to occur soon, endgame behavior should be less likely. Yet this strategy would be highly paternalistic and unfair to the employees and would be difficult to implement in an industry that faces strict and transparent termination dates. It would also pay little attention to the Swedish experience, which has highlighted the importance to safe operations of having transparent communication within the organization complemented by a monitoring system that attends to workers' psychological well-being (the "feeling of the workers").[43]

A possible response to the industry's difficulties in recruiting new talent would be to establish innovative engineering programs focusing on the decommissioning and dismantling of aging nuclear power plants. Given that 234 operating reactors worldwide are more than 30 years old and, of those, 64 are more than 40 years old,[44] there will be a fast-growing demand for this new and sophisticated expertise. Relatedly, the RSK has recommended implementing *strategic competence management*: a repertoire of measures with the goal of monitoring, maintaining, and further developing safety-relevant competences among employees in the nuclear power industry.[21] This approach also includes adopting measures (such as additional professional training and financial incentives) to counteract the ongoing loss of competence by fostering employees' commitment to their companies. At the same time, strategic competence management might also mean offering professional development and training in transferable skills to those employees who will inevitably have to transition to new careers in other industries, and perhaps even providing rewards for enrolling in the training.

Finally, on the level of public policymaking, decisionmakers need to recognize the challenge of designing and implementing phaseout policies that minimize the risk of endgame behavior. For instance, the Federal Council of Switzerland and the Swiss Parliament have decided to phase out nuclear energy gradually. Specifically, nuclear power plants will not be replaced once their operating lifetimes end. However, they can remain operational within their operating lifetime as long as their safety is guaranteed, that is, as long as a plant meets the statutory safety requirements. Such a phaseout policy provides a strong financial incentive to maintain and invest in high levels of safety and may thus be a more suitable way of keeping the risks of endgame behavior to a minimum—at least as long as some uncertainty remains regarding the onset of the decommissioning process.

author affiliations

Schöbel: University of Basel. Hertwig: Max Planck Institute for Human Development. Rieskamp: University of Basel. Corresponding author's e-mail: m.schoebel@unibas.ch.

author note

All authors contributed equally to the conduct of the experiments and the writing of the manuscript. We greatly appreciate the comments of Michael Baram and John S. Carroll on a previous version of the article. We thank Susannah Goss and Laura Wiles for editing the manuscript and Gilles Dutilh for preparing the figures. We also thank the Swedish Radiation Safety Authority for providing data on reported incidents in Swedish nuclear reactors.

supplemental material

- https://behavioralpolicy.org/publications/

- Methods & Analysis

endnote

A. From the editors to nonscientists: For any given data set, the statistical test used depends on the number of data points and the type of measurement being used, such as proportions or means. The p value of a statistical test is the probability of obtaining a result equal to or more extreme than would be observed merely by chance, assuming there are no true differences between groups under study (the null hypothesis). Researchers traditionally view $p < .05$ as statistically significant, with lower values indicating a stronger basis for rejecting the null hypothesis. The W score is the minimum of the sum of positive or negative signed ranks; the smaller its value (with a minimum of 0), the less likely it is that the result occurred by chance (assuming the null hypothesis).

references

1. Federal Ministry for the Environment, Nature Conservation and Nuclear Safety. (2002, February 1). *Atomausstiegsgesetz nimmt letzte Hürde* [Nuclear phase-out law takes the last hurdle; press release]. Retrieved from http://www.bmub.bund.de/presse/pressemitteilungen/pm/artikel/atomausstiegsgesetz-nimmt-letzte-huerde/

2. Federal Office for the Safety of Nuclear Waste Management. (2017). Laufzeiten deutscher Kernkraftwerke [Operating times of German nuclear power plants]. Retrieved from https://www.bfe.bund.de/DE/kt/kta-deutschland/kkw/laufzeiten/laufzeiten.html

3. von Neumann, J., & Morgenstern, O. (1944). *Theory of games and economic behavior.* Princeton, NJ: Princeton University Press.

4. Fudenberg, D., & Tirole, J. (1991). *Game theory.* Cambridge, MA: MIT Press.

5. Auman, R. J., & Maschler, R. (1995). *Repeated games with incomplete information.* Cambridge, MA: MIT Press.

6. Selten, R., & Stoecker, R. (1986). End behaviour in sequences of finite prisoner's dilemma supergames: A learning theory approach. *Journal of Economic Behavior & Organization, 7,* 47–70. doi:10.1016/0167-2681(86)90021-1

7. Roth, A. E., & Murnighan, J. K. (1978). Equilibrium behavior and repeated play of the prisoner's dilemma. *Journal of Mathematical Psychology, 17,* 189–198. doi:10.1016/0022-2496(78)90030-5

8. Andreoni, J. (1988). Why free ride? Strategies and learning in public goods experiments. *Journal of Public Economics, 37,* 291–304. doi:10.1016/0047-2727(88)90043-6

9. Fehr, E., & Gächter, S. (2002, January 10). Altruistic punishment in humans. *Nature, 415,* 137–140. doi:10.1038/415137a

10. Rasmussen, J. (1997). Risk management in a dynamic society: A modeling problem. *Safety Science, 27,* 183–213. doi:10.1016/s0925-7535(97)00052-0

11. Leveson, N. (2004). A new accident model for engineering safer systems. *Safety Science, 42,* 237–270. doi:10.1016/s0925-7535(03)00047-x

12. Leveson, N. (2011). Applying systems thinking to analyze and learn from events. *Safety Science, 49,* 55–64. doi:10.1016/j.ssci.2009.12.021

13. Gillis, J. (2014, September 13). Sun and wind alter global landscape, leaving utilities behind. *The New York Times.* Retrieved from http://www.nytimes.com/2014/09/14/science/earth/sun-and-wind-alter-german-landscape-leaving-utilities-behind.html?_r=0

14. Dohmen, F., & Hawranek, D. (2014, May 15). Bad banks for nuclear plants: Utilities look to German taxpayers. *Spiegel Online.* Retrieved from http://www.spiegel.de/international/germany/utility-companies-want-public-trust-for-winding-down-nuclear-plants-a-969707.html

15. Commission to Review the Financing for the Phase-out of Nuclear Energy. (2016). *Responsibility, safety and certainty—A new consensus on nuclear waste disposal: Final report of the Commission to Review the Financing for the Phase-out of Nuclear Energy.* Retrieved from https://www.bmwi.de/Redaktion/EN/Downloads/bericht-expertenkommission-kernenergie.pdf?__blob=publicationFile&v=2

16. E.ON and E.OUT: A German power-producer is breaking itself up to face the future. (2014, December 4). *The Economist.* Retrieved from http://www.economist.com/news/business/21635503-german-power-producer-breaking-itself-up-face-future-eon-and-eout

17. Chazan, G. (2016, March 15). Eon and RWE sue German government over nuclear shutdown. *Financial Times.* Retrieved from http://www.ft.com/cms/s/0/df44d1ee-e792-11e5-bc31-138df2ae9ee6.html#axzz4IQTrXd9s

18. Rueter, G. (2016, December 6). Opinion: Limiting the greed of the nuclear industry. Retrieved from Deutsche Welle website: http://www.dw.com/en/opinion-limiting-the-greed-of-the-nuclear-industry/a-36664176

19. Hellemans, A. (2014, November 12). Vattenfall seeks $6 billion in compensation for German nuclear phase-out. *IEEE Spectrum.* Retrieved from http://spectrum.ieee.org/energywise/energy/nuclear/swedish-energy-giant-vattenfall-nets-billions-for-nuclear-phaseout

20. Reactor Safety Commission. (2012, July 12). *Drohende Gefährdung der kerntechnischen Sicherheit durch Know-How- und Motivationsverlust* [Potential threats to nuclear safety through loss of know-how and motivation; memorandum]. Retrieved from http://www.rskonline.de/sites/default/files/reports/epanlagersk449hp.pdf

21. Reactor Safety Commission. (2016, November 3). *Monitoring von Know-how- und Motivationsverlust und geeignete Maßnahmen zur Stärkung von Motivation und Know-how-Erhalt in der deutschen Kernenergiebranche* [Monitoring of loss of know-how and motivation and suitable measures for strengthening motivation and preserving know-how in German nuclear power industries; statement]. Retrieved from http://www.rskonline.de/sites/default/files/reports/epanlage1rsk488hp_0.pdf

22. Schönberger, A. (2017, January 31). Areva ist Geschichte [Areva is history]. *Frankfurter Rundschau.* Retrieved from http://www.fr.de/rhein-main/offenbach-areva-ist-geschichte-a-743791

23. Kein Ergebnis: Gespräche über Lohnkürzung bei RWE [No result: Talks on wage cuts at RWE]. (2016, June 15). *Kölnische Rundschau.* Retrieved from http://www.rundschau-online.de/wirtschaft/kein-ergebnis-gespraeche-ueber-lohnkuerzung-bei-rwe-24232346

24. E.ON's nuclear unit to cut at least half its workforce by 2026. (2017, July 12). Retrieved from https://uk.reuters.com/article/eon-nuclear-jobs-idUKL8N1K31YL

25. Dehmer, D. (2016, March 7). Wie sicher ist der Atomausstieg? [How safe is the nuclear phase-out?]. *Der Tagesspiegel.* Retrieved from http://www.tagesspiegel.de/politik/atomkraftwerke-wie-sicher-ist-der-atomausstieg-/13061456.html

26. Sommer, S. (2016, August 3). Kerntechniker in der Klemme [Nuclear engineers under pressure]. *Frankfurter Allgemeine Zeitung.* Retrieved from http://www.faz.net/aktuell/beruf-chance/campus/macht-der-atomausstieg-ein-kernenergie-studium-ueberfluessig-14362056.html

27. Probst, T. M., & Brubaker, T. L. (2001). The effects of job insecurity on employee safety outcomes: Cross-sectional and longitudinal explorations. *Journal of Occupational Health Psychology, 6,* 139–159. doi:10.1037/1076-8998.6.2.139

28. Probst, T. M. (2004). Safety and insecurity: Exploring the moderating effect of organizational safety climate. *Journal of Occupational Health Psychology, 9,* 3–10. doi:10.1037/1076-8998.9.1.3

29. Sutton, R. I. (1987). The process of organizational death: Disbanding and reconnecting. *Administrative Science Quarterly, 32,* 542–569. doi:10.2307/2392883

30. Weick, K., & Sutcliffe, K. (2001). *Managing the unexpected: Assuring high performance in an age of complexity.* San Fransisco, CA: Jossey-Bass.

31. International Nuclear Advisory Group. (1991). *Safety culture* (Safety Series No. 75-INSAG-4). Vienna, Austria: International Atomic Energy Agency.

32. Federal Office for the Safety of Nuclear Waste Management. (2016). Reporting procedure. Retrieved from http://www.bfe.bund.de/EN/ns/events/reporting-procedure/reporting-procedure_node.html

33. Ministry of the Environment. (1998). *Sweden's first national report under the convention on nuclear safety: Swedish implementation of the obligations of the convention* (Ds 1998:54). Retrieved from http://www.regeringen.se/49c6b3/contentassets/625f71ce5da644549043ffe124e44590convention-on-nuclear-safety-ds-1998-54.pdf

34. Wiwen-Nilsson, T. (2006). Phasing-out of nuclear power in Sweden. *Journal of Energy & Natural Resources Law, 24,* 355–361. doi:10.1080/02646811.2006.11433441

35. Hansson, M., & Wigblad, R. (2006). Pyrrhic victories—Anticipating the closedown effect. *The International Journal of Human Resource Management, 17,* 938–958. doi:10.1080/09585190600641255

36. Carroll, J. S. (1998). Organizational learning activities in high-hazard industries: The logics underlying self-analysis. *Journal of Management Studies, 35,* 699–717. doi:10.1111/1467-6486.00116

37. Plott, C. R., & Smith, V. L. (2008). *Handbook of experimental economics results* (Vol. 1). Amsterdam, the Netherlands: Elsevier.

38. Binmore, K., & Klemperer, P. (2002). The biggest auction ever: The sale of the British 3G telecom licenses. *The Economic Journal, 112*(478), C74–C96. doi:10.1111/1468-0297.00020

39. Slovic, P. (1987, April 17). Perception of risk. *Science, 236,* 280–285. doi:10.1126/science.3563507

40. Roeser, S. (2011). Nuclear energy, risk, and emotions. *Philosophy & Technology, 24,* 197–201. doi:10.1007/s13347-011-0027-6

41. Federal Ministry for the Environment, Nature Conservation, Building and Nuclear Safety. (2016). *Convention on Nuclear Safety: Report by the Government of the Federal Republic of Germany for the Seventh Review Meeting in March/April 2017.* Retrieved from https://doris.bfs.de/jspui/bitstream/urn:nbn:de:0221-2016100614132/1/CNS_Bericht_2017_en_bf.pdf

42. Folger, R. (1993). Reactions to mistreatment at work. In J. K. Murnighan (Ed.), *Social psychology in organizations: Advances in theory and research* (pp. 161–183). Englewood Cliffs, NJ: Prentice Hall.

43. International Atomic Energy Agency. (2003). *Managing the early termination of operation of nuclear power plants* (Safety Reports Series No. 31). Vienna, Austria: Author.

44. Schneider, M., & Froggatt, A. (2017). *World Nuclear Industry Status Report 2017.* Mycle Schneider Consulting. Retrieved from https://www.worldnuclearreport.org/IMG/pdf/20170912wnisr2017-en-lr.pdf

Regulating for
ethical culture

Linda K. Treviño, Jonathan Haidt, & Azish E. Filabi

abstract

Recent cases of corporate fraud have heightened regulatory interest in leveraging organizational culture to encourage ethical behavior. Policymakers in government and industry wish to use culture to enhance the enforcement-based approaches that they have historically relied on, but they want guidance on how to proceed. In this article, we review the organizational behavior literature on ethical culture. We define the components of ethical culture in organizations and summarize research into how to assess and strengthen it. We demonstrate that assessment must be an integral part of regulatory efforts to strengthen ethical culture, and we recommend that policymakers encourage industries to use standardized, validated measures to further policy goals.

Treviño, L. K., Haidt, J., & Filabi, A. E. (2017). Regulating for ethical culture. *Behavioral Science & Policy, 3*(2), 57–70.

The 1980s are generally remembered as a boom time on Wall Street, with rising market indices and plenty of fraud. The movie *Wall Street* encapsulated the period in the character of Gordon Gekko, with his "greed is good" mantra. The era also brought the savings and loan crisis, which required costly government bailouts of financial institutions, some of which had engaged in pervasive fraud.

Suppose that in 1990, the Justice Department had tasked a team of lawyers and economists with crafting a regulatory approach that would improve the ethical behavior of corporations, especially financial companies. The result would probably look something like the Federal Sentencing Guidelines for Organizations (FSGO), which were published by the U.S. Sentencing Commission in 1991.[1]

The carrot-and-stick approach that the commission adopted incentivized companies to put personnel and procedures in place to guide employee conduct, encourage reporting of misconduct, and monitor and punish wrongdoing. Firms that developed ethics and compliance (E&C) programs that could "prevent and detect violations of law"[1] effectively would benefit by receiving lighter penalties and shorter probation periods if their employees were later discovered to have committed criminal offenses. The FSGO outlined the commission's expectations for reasonable components of E&C programs, including periodic risk assessments, due diligence (with respect to hiring individuals and undertaking periodic evaluations of its E&C program), and an obligation to report the results of assessments.

Since 1991, most large companies have established E&C programs. Many in the regulatory community, however, remain skeptical that the programs are working as the authors of the FSGO intended. They fear that too many are "check-the-box" programs that make it seem like a company is making an effort (by establishing policies and procedures that look good on paper) when, in fact, many employees perceive that the programs are mere window dressing.

In 2004, recognizing that many E&C programs appeared to adhere to the letter of the guidelines but were not seriously integrated into daily organizational life, the U.S. Sentencing Commission revised the FSGO so that companies were obliged to "promote an organizational culture that encourages ethical conduct and a commitment to compliance with the law."[2] This new element, however, left companies and regulators to wonder, How does one create an ethical culture and assess whether a company's culture encourages ethical conduct?

In this article, we offer answers to those questions. In the first section, we provide context, surveying current regulatory initiatives that encourage companies to embrace ethical culture through E&C programs and other measures. Next, we outline the complex systems that constitute an ethical culture, integrating insights from anthropology and the organizational-behavior literature specific to ethical culture. In the final sections, we review the literature on ethical culture assessment and offer recommendations for how to regulate ethical culture in organizations.

Recent Regulatory Interest in Culture

The FSGO remains the main source of guidance for organizations creating internal E&C programs. In recent years, the regulatory and enforcement community, particularly in the financial industry, has come to agree with its stance that creating an ethical culture is key to an organization's successful compliance with regulations. Notably, in October 2014, William Dudley, the president of the Federal Reserve Bank of New York, convened the heads of U.S. financial institutions for the first of a series of Reforming Culture and Behavior in the Financial Services Industry conferences. This meeting occurred at a time of intense scrutiny of the financial industry: in the wake of the global financial crisis of 2008, the Bernard Madoff Ponzi scheme (2008/2009), the J.P. Morgan Chase "London whale" trading scandal (2012), and revelations of collusion by financial institutions in setting the London Interbank Offered

Core Findings

What is the issue?
Assessing and regulating ethical culture in organizations is important for preventing fraud and costly cases of misconduct. In order to know where to begin, however, leaders and policymakers need to know how E&C orientation, leadership, climate, fairness, and trust feed into actionable assessments of ethical culture.

How can you act?
Selected recommendations include:
1) Creating an independent third-party organization to serve as a neutral research entity that conducts assessments of ethical culture, communicating between the industry and regulators
2) Monitoring how an organization's ethical culture changes over time in a process of continual learning and experimentation

Who should take the lead?
Regulators and industry leaders, organizational psychologists, behavioral science researchers

Rate (better known as LIBOR; 2012), among others.

Dudley made a strong case for the importance of measuring and improving ethical culture. He began by rejecting claims that these scandals could generally be pinned on one or a few rogue traders or bad apples. He then gave a succinct definition of organizational culture and argued that the behavior of senior management is critical to establishing ethical norms:

> Culture exists within every firm whether it is recognized or ignored, whether it is nurtured or neglected, and whether it is embraced or disavowed. *Culture reflects the prevailing attitudes and behaviors within a firm. It is how people react not only to black and white, but to all of the shades of grey* [emphasis added]. . . .

> As a first step, senior leaders need to hold up a mirror to their own behavior and critically examine behavioral norms at their firm. . . .

> Firms must take a comprehensive approach to improving their culture that encompasses recruitment, onboarding, career development, performance reviews, pay and promotion.[3]

Dudley then urged the assembled chiefs of financial institutions to develop a common approach to measuring an organization's culture, beginning with an anonymous employee survey:

> An important measurement of progress is employees' assessment of their firm's culture. To this end, we encourage the industry . . . to develop a comprehensive culture survey. This anonymous survey would be fielded across firms each year by an independent third-party and the results shared with supervisors. Having a common survey instrument would promote benchmarking of, and accountability for, progress on culture and behavior.[3]

(Researchers have developed some survey tools, which we describe later. So far, though, most industries lack standardized measures for their fields.)

Other banking regulators, including the Financial Industry Regulatory Authority (the self-regulatory organization for broker-dealers also known as FINRA) and the Office of the Comptroller of the Currency (OCC), have likewise turned their attention to culture as a lever to improve ethical behavior in organizations. In January 2016, FINRA's annual Regulatory and Examinations Priorities Letter[4] to the firms it oversees asked them to report on how they monitor the implementation of and compliance with the firm's cultural values.

The OCC has taken a slightly different approach and put responsibility directly on the banks' executives and boards of directors to integrate the oversight of corporate culture into their duties. The July 2016 *Comptroller's Handbook: Corporate and Risk Governance*,[5] which serves as the guidance document for OCC bank examiners (and thus communicates regulatory expectations to the firms), states that it is the duty of the board and senior management to "promote a sound corporate culture." The handbook lists a series of expected undertakings by the C-suite (that is, the company board and senior management) to this end, including ensuring that the appropriate behaviors are "linked to performance reviews and compensation practices" and that managers "integrate the culture into the bank's strategic planning process and risk management practices."

Clearly, regulators are increasingly focusing on using corporate culture as a tool to prevent misconduct. And they continue to have their work cut out for them, as the ethics scandals of the past couple of years make clear. Recall when, for example, Wells Fargo employees opened accounts for customers without their knowledge or consent,[6] and Volkswagen engineers installed software designed to fool regulators into thinking that the company's vehicles met emission standards.[7] To be successful, regulators need a deep understanding of exactly what an ethical culture looks like, as well as how

---

that culture can be assessed, reported on, and managed within large, complex organizations.

Regulators would also be wise to familiarize themselves with psychology. Just as economists have expanded their thinking about the drivers of financial interactions to include behavioral economics, regulators interested in enhancing ethical behavior in corporations should read more psychological research, particularly work exploring the drivers of ethical and unethical behavior in organizations. The behavioral ethics literature generally defines *ethical behavior* as activity that is consistent with society's accepted moral norms,[8] and studies found in the literature typically focus on behavior that breaches those norms (for example, cheating, lying, and stealing).

The realms of ethical and legally compliant behaviors overlap to a large extent, because the law represents general agreement in society about what constitutes right and appropriate behavior. However, many of the ethical and unethical behaviors found in organizations simply are not addressed by law and regulation (such as certain conflicts of interest) or have not yet been addressed (such as whether new information technology is being used ethically). Therefore, decisions about what is ethical or unethical reside in a gray area that is open to discussion and social consensus within organizations and society as a whole.

Because organizational culture is being targeted as a tool for managing ethical conduct in organizations, those who are charged with managing and regulating it need to have a firm grasp of what an ethical culture looks like. We now step back to examine its features in detail.

What Is Ethical Culture?

The word *culture* comes from the Latin word *cultura,* which means cultivation or tillage. The agricultural origin of the word conveys the sense of shaping or nurturing something over time. Like plants, people are rooted in a particular place, and they are shaped by the norms of that place. For example, when employees show up for work in a new organization, they quickly get a sense of "how things are done around here" and what kinds of behaviors are accepted and expected.

Culture has been the central concept in anthropology for over a century, and anthropologists have taken the lead in defining the term. Writing in 1995, Richard Shweder, one of the founders of modern cultural psychology, gave this definition:

> Culture is a reality lit up by a morally enforceable conceptual scheme composed of values (desirable goals) and causal beliefs (including ideas about means-ends connections) that is exemplified or instantiated in practice.[9]

Shweder's definition notes that culture is more than conceptual schemes and beliefs: it envelops people and creates a reality that is expressed and passed on to others by the practices and rituals of the group. Most important, Shweder's definition explicitly recognizes the role of morality in enforcing the group's ways of thinking and acting. A company's moral norms can lead employees to engage in upright behavior, but only if socially beneficial behavior is what is modeled. If the culture includes unethical practices, such as cheating customers, then going along with those practices can seem like a moral necessity to insiders. An employee who violates the implicit rules of the culture by exposing its practices to outsiders—or who just tries to change it from within—may face criticism, shaming, and ostracism. For such reasons, social psychologists generally focus on the "bad barrel" rather than on individual "bad apples" when they study wrongdoing in organizations.[10]

Shweder's approach aligns with the definition of ethical culture in organizations that one of us (Treviño) has used for years: if culture can be thought of as "how we do things around here," then ethical culture is the employees' understanding of "how we do things around here in relation to ethics."[11] More specifically, an organization's ethical culture is a complex system with multiple moving components that constantly send messages to employees that either support or do not support ethical conduct. The behaviors of leaders and the activities carried out through a company's systems for managing and improving employee performance are just two powerful examples of an organization's activities sending signals, both formal and informal, to employees about an organization's ethical culture.

Regulators and corporate leaders also need to understand that ethical culture is not an objective truth. Rather, it comprises the messages that employees perceive they are getting and that they are acting on every day, not necessarily the messages that management intends to convey. An organization's efforts to study and improve its culture must therefore include direct questions asking its employees for their perceptions of the multiple aspects of ethical culture.

In a perfectly ethical culture (a rare bird), all of the culture components consistently send a clear message that ethical conduct is expected. Employees are recruited on the basis of and then socialized into a set of aspirational values, rules, and codes that are designed to guide behavior in the gray areas. These are upheld every day by communications from leaders and by role models and are supported by a reward and discipline system that sends consistent messages about expectations and accountability. In a perfectly unethical culture (also rare, thankfully), all of the culture components send a clear message that unethical conduct is expected and rewarded. Employees find that they need to get with the program or leave. Most organizations, however, fall in between these two extremes. Employees receive mixed messages from different components of the culture, leaving them to make sense of what

"If the culture includes unethical practices, such as cheating customers, then going along with those practices can seem like a moral necessity to insiders"

behaviors are expected of them and what they should and should not do. These cultures are in need of assessment and intervention just as much as perfectly unethical cultures are.

Figure 1 depicts the constituents of an organization's ethical culture. Employee behavior is influenced by the messages received from formal and informal cultural systems. The formal systems include the official communications and actions of the executive leadership, employee selection systems, policies and codes, orientation and training systems, performance management systems, organizational authority (hierarchy) structures, and decisionmaking processes. The informal systems consist of role models (managers at all levels), norms of daily behavior, rituals that help members understand the organization's identity and what it values, myths and stories people tell about the organization, and the language people use in daily behavior.

Note that the tone set at the top of an organization trickles down to influence all other

Figure 1. Components of an ethical organizational culture

Formal Systems	Informal Systems
Executive Leadership	Role Models and Heroes
Employee Selection Systems	Norms
Policies and Codes	Rituals
Orientation and Training Systems	Myths and Stories
Performance Management Systems	Language
Organizational Authority Structures	
Decisionmaking Processes	

elements, including leadership at lower levels. Senior leaders are critical to establishing an ethical culture—they provide resources for effective programs, send values-based messages, and serve as role models for ethical behavior and the use of ethical language. They have the potential to influence every other system within the organization.

Critically, leaders also need to attend to the alignment of the organization's cultural systems. When all of the constituent systems support ethical behavior, the company will have an ethical culture, although it needs constant attention to keep it that way. When the culture is in a state of misalignment—when cultural systems send mixed messages—the company is less likely to have an ethical culture. For example, employees pay close attention to what the performance management system rewards; many employees will assume that messages about bottom-line performance are the real messages they should be attending to, and they will behave accordingly.

The most direct way to evaluate ethical culture is to measure employee perceptions of both the formal and the informal systems and the alignment or the misalignment of those messages. Next, we discuss methods for assessing culture in organizations, and we present evidence that using and tracking those measures can lead to more effective E&C programs.

How to Assess Ethical Culture: The Big Picture

One important guideline for assessing ethical culture is that success depends on corporate policymakers, including the chief executive officer (CEO) and the board of a company, being driving forces in the process. In many organizations, a chief ethics officer advocates for ethical culture assessments, but for an assessment effort to be effective, senior leadership's full support must be clear. The effort must also have the backing of other internal stakeholders, such as the human resources department.

Although CEOs have a crucial role to play, most do not have the time to also be the chief ethics officer. Yet, like a garden, an ethical culture must be constantly tended. An organizational leader with credibility and authority needs to be thinking about and nurturing the organization's ethical culture every day and ensuring that weeds and pests do not begin to take over—something that can happen very quickly, unraveling all that has been so carefully built over time. This role should fall to a highly respected ethics officer who has the full support of the CEO and the board (as well as an independent relationship with the board). Then the CEO must model the right behaviors, provide resources for building and sustaining ethical culture, and consistently back the endeavor by aligning internal systems.

Executives in upper management must also recognize that their own perceptions of the organization's ethical culture are almost certainly rosier than are the perceptions of rank-and-file employees. Research indicates that top managers are often the last to know about an unethical or misaligned culture.[12] Their elevated status may render them oblivious, or their people may be unwilling to tell them what is really going on. Bad news does not travel up very effectively in most organizations. Recent research also suggests that higher ranking employees are less likely to engage in principled dissent—to report and act on unethical behaviors they observe—perhaps because they identify so much with the organization.[13] So it is essential that managers recognize their own limitations and biases and rely on good data that are based on employee perceptions at all levels of the organizational hierarchy. It is a safe bet that lower level employees are the ones who know what is really happening in an organization.

The tools chosen to assess an organization's culture are also critical. Unethical behavior is difficult to observe because it is purposely kept hidden. Therefore, anonymous surveys and focus groups (often in combination) have been the assessment methods of choice. Done right, those approaches are useful. What does not work is relying on compliance officers who simply note the existence of program elements (such as an employee orientation program

1991

Year in which the U.S. Sentencing Commission published the Federal Sentencing Guidelines for Organizations (FSGO)

E&C

Corporate Ethics and Compliance program responses to the FSGO

2004

FSGO revised to include ethical culture

"if regulators access the underlying data generated by assessments, then respondents will be motivated to influence, alter, or withhold the results of assessments"

that describes the company's values and an accompanying training program on the code of conduct) or including a couple of broad ethics-related questions on the annual employee survey. Unfortunately, the latter is what many organizations are currently doing, if they are doing anything at all to assess whether their culture is ethical.

As Dudley urged in 2014, companies should use a validated, reliable, and standardized way of assessing "how we do things around here" with regard to ethics.[3] Yet having the right tools alone is not enough. Who conducts the assessment and who can access the data can influence whether the final data are informative and used appropriately. The regulatory challenge, however, is that if regulators access the underlying data generated by assessments, then respondents will be motivated to influence, alter, or withhold the results of assessments. Bodies that regulate an industry should therefore create incentives for the industry to create an independent third-party organization to serve as a neutral research entity that conducts assessments and facilitates communication of their results between the industry and regulators. The regulatory stick in this instance can be penalties against companies that do not participate in such industry initiatives.

We know of two effective models of industry-based self-governance organizations: (a) the Defense Industry Initiative on Business Conduct and Ethics, comprising 77 signatory companies that are U.S. Defense Department contractors,[14] and (b) the U.K. Banking Standards Board, created after the global financial crisis to promote high standards of behavior and competence across the banking industry in the United Kingdom and currently comprising 31 member companies.[15] Neither of these was created because of a law or regulation, although the U.K. Banking Standards Board was a response to

recommendations made by the Parliamentary Commission on Banking Standards.

The standardization of assessment tools is important because it can enable companies in an industry to compare their results against those of other firms of the same size and circumstances. Such comparisons are helpful because firms in the same industry are likely to face similar ethical issues and circumstances (such as the regulatory environment). Standardization also encourages voluntary sharing of information across organizations, quickening the pace of learning about what works to improve culture. Moreover, standardization allows companies to measure their ethical culture against their own ethical aspirations, values, and goals, and it can provide longitudinal data to indicate whether new ethics-promoting policies and interventions are working as planned.

Some of the top academic researchers in behavioral ethics have already developed many of the tools necessary to assess the various features of an ethical culture; those features and tools are reviewed in the next section. We recommend the measures described there, which are drawn from published analyses, because they have been validated using sophisticated psychometric procedures that ensure the approaches can accurately and reliably measure what they are intended to measure.

Ideally, companies would assess employee perceptions of all components of the multisystem framework that constitutes ethical culture, as described in Figure 1. Validated survey measures do not yet exist in the literature for every component, however. To address this gap, Ethical Systems, where one of us (Filabi) works and two of us (Treviño and Haidt) participate as Steering Committee members, has convened the Ethical Systems Culture Measurement Working Group. The group, consisting of prominent behavioral ethics researchers, is conducting research to develop the needed assessment tools. (See note A.) The data collected in the project will be used to study the relationships among elements of ethical culture and to determine their relative effects on important outcomes, such as observed unethical conduct and the likelihood that employees will report problems to management. Future phases of the project will include additional modules on other aspects of the multisystem framework of ethical culture.

Past research has uncovered ways to increase the truthfulness of survey results. Employees are likely to complete surveys and do so honestly if they know their responses are anonymous, if they trust that their responses will not be traced back to them, and if they believe that the results will be used for a good purpose. Hence, it is extremely important to have a trusted third party collect and manage the data, delivering results to management that do not identify individuals. Obviously, if employees view management as corrupt, they may distrust anyone brought in by management. And employees who are benefiting from a corrupt environment will probably be dishonest to maintain the status quo. But, in our experience, most employees would prefer to work for an ethical organization, will participate, and will provide truthful feedback.

Survey administrators can further increase the trustworthiness of the results by including a measure of social desirability bias (the tendency to give answers that employees perceive researchers or managers want to hear) and by controlling for that bias statistically in the data analysis. Social desirability bias can also be minimized by asking about observed unethical conduct (for example, by asking, "How frequently have you observed a certain kind of unethical behavior in the organization during the past year?") rather than by having employees report on their own unethical conduct. Employees are more honest when reporting on observations.

As long as individuals are not identifiable, it is also helpful to collect and analyze data in a way that enables the organization to learn whether the members in a unit agree that the unit has

ethical culture problems. Ideally, units with such problems can be spotted and their problems addressed. For example, by examining unit-level data, a firm could learn that a particular division has a more unethical culture than other divisions do, suggesting a need for intervention. At that point, focus groups might be convened to delve more deeply into issues that surface in the survey. Trusted outsiders can also be brought in to run these focus groups and thereby assure employee anonymity. Results of surveys and focus groups (the good, the bad, and the ugly) should be shared with employees, along with plans for intervention, so that they know the results are being taken seriously.

How to Assess Ethical Culture: The Nuts & Bolts

Employee perceptions of the following five aspects of ethical culture have a profound effect on their behavior. Assessing these perceptions can reveal where interventions and changes are most needed.

1. Orientation of E&C Programs

In 1999, Treviño and colleagues carried out a large-scale study to investigate which aspects of E&C programs support or interfere with an organization's goals for ethical behavior.[16] They administered a survey to more than 10,000 randomly selected employees at all hierarchical levels in six large U.S. companies across a variety of industries. Their results have important implications for how policymakers should define the effectiveness of E&C programs, as well as for how companies should manage such programs.

In the study, they assessed program effectiveness by focusing on seven outcomes that are relevant to the success of any E&C program (see Table 1 for the complete list of desired outcomes). The investigators concluded that, among other elements, an effective E&C program is one that reduces observations of misbehavior, increases awareness of ethical issues, and increases the likelihood that employees will speak up about problems to managers as well as report misbehavior via other channels established by the company.

Table 1. What is an effective ethics & compliance program?

Effective ethics and compliance programs achieve the outcomes listed below. Program effectiveness can be evaluated in part through surveys of employees. Assessments often ask respondents to rate statements on a sliding scale. The sample items here come from a survey developed by Linda K. Treviño and her colleagues.[A] Outcomes 2 through 7 are evaluated using a 5-point scale that ranges from *strongly disagree* (1) to *strongly agree* (5).

Program outcomes	Sample survey items
1. Reduced observations of unethical and illegal behaviors.	On a scale of 1 (*never*) to 5 (*very frequently*), indicate how often have you observed each of the behaviors listed below during the past year: (A list of 32 behaviors can be adjusted to best fit the needs of the organization. Examples of behaviors to evaluate include lying to customers, padding an expense account, falsifying financial reports, giving kickbacks, stealing from the company, and misusing insider information.)
2. Increased employee awareness of ethical and legal issues that arise at work.	Employees in this company are quick to notice when a situation raises ethics or compliance issues.
3. Creation of conditions that increase employee willingness to seek ethical and legal advice within the company.	When ethical issues arise, employees look for advice within the company.
4. Increased employee willingness to report bad news to management.	Employees here are comfortable delivering bad news to their managers.
5. Increased employee willingness to report ethical violations to management, such as via ethics hotlines (often anonymous) and other reporting channels.	If someone here knew that a coworker was doing something unethical, he or she would report it to management.
6. Increased employee perception that the program is contributing to better (and more ethical) decisionmaking in the organization.	People in this firm make more effective ethical decisions because of the ethics and/or compliance activities that are in place.
7. Increased employee commitment to the organization.	I feel attached to the company because of its values.

A. Treviño, L. K., Weaver, G. R., Gibson, D. G., & Toffler, B. L. (1999). Managing ethics and legal compliance: What works and what hurts. *California Management Review, 41*(2), 131–151.

Treviño et al. also found that employee perceptions of program orientation are extremely important to the outcomes of any E&C program.[16] The researchers identified four orientation categories: (a) values based, rooted in self-governance and intrinsic motivation; (b) compliance based, focused primarily on preventing, detecting, and punishing legal and policy violations; (c) external stakeholder based, focused on maintaining relationships with customers, the community, suppliers, and others; and (d) protection based, focused on shielding top management from blame in the face of legal or ethical problems. To assess employee perceptions of program orientation, Treviño et al. asked survey respondents to choose from a list of goals to indicate what they believed the company's E&C policies and activities were designed to accomplish (for instance, support employee goals and aspirations, encourage shared values, or detect unethical employees). The researchers then determined whether and how strongly those responses each correlated with the criteria for effectiveness—the desired program outcomes, as described in Table 1.

The programs that employees perceived to have a values-based orientation scored highest on each of the seven effectiveness criteria in Table 1. Compliance-based and external-stakeholder-based orientations were not as powerful but were still helpful. The researchers also found a clear marker of a bad program: employee perception that the E&C program was oriented toward protecting top management from blame. When the protection-based orientation was perceived, more unethical or illegal behaviors were observed, employees were less aware

"self-interested ethical climates increase unethical behaviors"

of ethical issues, and employees were less likely to seek advice about ethical concerns.[16]

In practice, the program orientation of most companies is probably best described as a hybrid. The data suggest that a primarily but not entirely values-based orientation can nonetheless be highly effective at improving ethical behavior if it is backed up with accountability systems and discipline for rule violators (elements that tend to be emphasized in compliance-based orientations).

2. Ethical Leadership

Treviño et al. also found that leadership is one of the strongest drivers of ethical culture.[16] In a later study, published in 2005, Michael Brown, Treviño, and David Harrison developed a model of ethical leadership that builds on Albert Bandura's social learning theory, which focuses on how people learn by observing others.[17] To influence followers' ethical behavior, they found, leaders must be credible and legitimate role models and be able to influence others, and they must model correct behavior by behaving ethically, communicating about ethics, setting high ethical standards, and holding employees accountable to those standards.

How can policymakers assess whether an organization has ethical leaders? Brown et al. developed an empirically validated 10-item Ethical Leadership Scale[17] that has since been used in many studies to show that ethical leadership correlates with increases in employee satisfaction, commitment to the organization, citizenship behavior, and willingness to report problems to management, as well as in a reduction in unethical behavior. Most of this research has been conducted among middle levels of management, supporting the idea that direct supervisors are at the front lines of building and sustaining an ethical culture.

3. Ethical Climate

In 2012, Anke Arnaud and Marshall Schminke published a paper on the role of egoism in shaping organizational ethics—that is, in establishing an ethical climate that is either self-interested or other-interested.[18] They developed and validated a 20-item instrument to measure ethical climate, as well as empathy and efficacy. To assess climate, they had employees rate their agreement with such statements as "People in my organization/department are very concerned about what is best for them personally," "People around here are mostly out for themselves," and "People in my department are actively concerned about their peers' interests."

Their research built on earlier work by Bart Victor and John B. Cullen[19] and by Kelly D. Martin and Cullen[20] on ethical workplace climates, which demonstrated that self-interested ethical climates increase unethical behaviors (such as theft, lying on or falsifying reports, accepting bribes, and employee deviance) and that the inverse is also true—that nonegoistic (benevolent) climates positively influence ethical outcomes.

In their 2012 study, Arnaud and Schminke found, however, that an ethical climate alone may be insufficient to lead to ethical behavior.[18] In other words, when employees generally agree on the right thing to do, the organization may not see a reduction in unethical behavior unless employees also collectively feel empathy toward the target of their behavior (such as the client, other employees, or other stakeholders) and believe they have the capacity to influence outcomes through their own actions (efficacy). The evidence showed that assessing employee perceptions of their colleagues' empathy and efficacy provides a more complete picture of how strongly the informal norms of an organization can reduce misbehavior. (See note B.)

4. Fairness

Treviño et al. determined in 1999 that fair treatment of employees is another important aspect of culture—as would be expected, given that organizational justice affects so many elements of day-to-day work, including compensation, promotion, and perceptions of whether all voices are heard equally. They reported that employees' perceptions of general fairness within an organization (as indicated by responses to statements such as "This organization treats its employees fairly"); fairness of rewards and punishments; and whether supervisors treat employees with courtesy, dignity, and respect all strongly correlated with each of the outcomes described in Table 1.[16] The two strongest correlations were between perceptions of fairness and (a) an employee's commitment to the organization and (b) an employee's willingness to deliver bad news to management.

These findings are consistent with those of recent research by Maureen Ambrose and Schminke.[21] Ambrose and Schminke developed the Perceived Overall Justice (POJ) scale, a six-item survey that asks employees to rate their agreement with three statements related to their perceptions of fair treatment (such as "Overall, I'm treated fairly by my organization") and three statements related to the organization more generally (such as "Overall, this organization treats its employees fairly"). The researchers found statistically significant correlations between POJ scores and outcomes such as employee job satisfaction, commitment to the organization, and intention to leave. They also found strong correlations with outcomes that were not self-reported—such as supervisors' assessments of how well employees performed on a task, whether they were good organizational citizens, and whether they engaged in behaviors that were harmful to the organization (organizational deviance).

5. Trust

The decision to trust another person or a company and its products is often based on a calculation of the trustworthiness of the other party. Measures of trust have been developed on the basis of the theory that a decision to trust can be assessed by considering an individual's willingness to be vulnerable and thus take the risk of putting faith in the other party. In 2006, David Schoorman and Gary Ballinger developed a seven-item scale to assess an employee's willingness to trust a supervisor.[22,23] The scale integrates constructs relating to the supervisor's ability, benevolence, and integrity. Sample statements rated by employees include "If my supervisor asked why a problem occurred, I would speak freely even if I were partly to blame"; "It is important for me to have a good way to keep an eye on my supervisor"; and "Increasing my vulnerability to criticism by my supervisor would be a mistake."

Evidence shows that trust pays. That is, high-trust environments result in more efficiency, more employee engagement, and better financial performance for organizations.[24,25]

How to Regulate Ethical Culture

We started this article by noting that regulators want guidance on how to assess whether companies have an ethical culture. Further, they want to be able to judge whether efforts to enhance ethical culture are translating into E&C programs that, in fact, increase ethical behavior.

Regulators can begin to address the first need by requiring companies to assess the state of their ethical culture regularly through surveys of employees, preferably ones that are standardized for the relevant industry. Although regulators cannot and should not attempt to mandate what the culture should be at a firm, they can require that each firm study its own culture to assess how the culture could be contributing to misconduct by employees and management. For example, if employees indicate that they are unlikely to report the misconduct they observe, because they do not believe management will take any action on their reports or they fear retaliation, regulators should expect that the organization will take that information seriously, search for root causes of the problems, and act to change systems that encourage such behavior and accompanying perceptions. Policymakers (including those who determine internal corporate policies) should also carefully consider who should have access to the results of culture assessments. On the one hand, access by regulators could incentivize firms to try to game the system or could make employees less forthcoming about their opinions; on the other hand, without regulatory pressure, many firms may be unwilling or unlikely to delve deeply into their ethical cultures.

Once baseline measures are in hand, firms should be encouraged to design interventions, monitor how their ethical culture changes over time, and determine whether targeted interventions are working. Companies can develop a process of continual learning and experimentation. For example, the baseline culture data can be used to understand the impact of various internal or external initiatives at the firm—such as whether revising compensation plans improves or damages ethical culture, whether a revamped training program alters employee perceptions of the culture, or whether the addition of an ombudsman program changes perceptions of the safety of speaking up.

To determine whether all these activities result in E&C programs that increase ethical behavior, policymakers can begin by encouraging companies and regulators to use the outcomes that indicate effectiveness provided in Table 1 and supplement those with additional outcomes that are particularly relevant for them. Ideally, a firm would also use internal data to measure ethical behavior, such as the firm's pending (defense) litigation matters, the frequency and underlying causes of regulatory enforcement actions by regulators, human resources data on the amount and kinds of reported misconduct, and the number of ethics-hotline calls made by employees and customers (although tying hotline calls to E&C effectiveness can be challenging).

Many in the E&C field have considered it extremely difficult to determine program effectiveness, because an effective program should prevent problems, and one cannot measure problems that have been avoided. They are right to an extent, but we have shown in this article that ethical culture can be assessed, interventions can be designed, and progress in outcomes can be monitored. The combination of self-reported survey data and other internal data can reveal how the firm's E&C program and culture are influencing outcomes. A more effective program would be associated with positive outcomes (such as an increased willingness of employees to deliver bad news to management) and negatively correlated with negative outcomes (such as pending defense litigation or regulatory enforcement actions).

Conclusion

Would assessments of ethical culture over time have prevented recent corporate scandals, such as those at Wells Fargo or Volkswagen? Yes, but only if employees reported honestly and senior management and the boards of directors gave those assessments credence and took serious action. Leaders who tend the ethical culture garden notice when weeds are sprouting and spreading. If the leaders at Wells Fargo and Volkswagen had done that, senior management would have been more attuned to the profound effects of their statements, actions, and policies on their employees. They would have been more aware of how their unattainable performance goals were being pursued unethically at lower levels. As ethical leaders, they would have been more approachable and open to input about the inability to achieve, without fraud, the very demanding goals that were set at the top. Middle managers and employees would have felt more empowered to speak up (anonymously, if necessary), and, in an ethical culture, their concerns would have been taken seriously.

Government policymakers and regulators should attend to the above recommendations for how to conduct assessments of culture and should integrate those assessments into their regulatory processes. Corporate policymakers, such as the CEO and board members, should also integrate ethical culture assessment into their efforts to proactively manage ethics and to use ethical culture as a lever to increase ethical conduct throughout their organizations. (For further discussion, see Policies That Encourage the Create of Ethical Organizational Culture.)

Researchers have learned a lot about conceptualizing and measuring ethical culture in organizations, but much more work remains to be done. For example, in this article, we have emphasized survey approaches. A full understanding of ethical culture, however, would also require qualitative approaches, such as

Policies That Encourage the Creation of Ethical Organizational Culture

To increase ethical behavior in organizations, policymakers and regulators should encourage organizations to undertake the following measures:

- **Assess ethical culture regularly.** A culture assessment, which evaluates perceptions of norms and behaviors, should be carried out in addition to an assessment of employee perceptions of the formal ethics and compliance (E&C) program. Use standardized and validated surveys that measure employee perceptions of the ethical orientation of E&C programs, ethical leadership, the fairness of the organization, and the trustworthiness of the company and its leaders, among other factors. Industries should consider having a trusted third party conduct sector-specific surveys, a method that can increase the honesty of the respondents.

  The Defense Industry Initiative (DII) on Business Ethics and Conduct, which represents several dozen companies that contract for the government, has worked for years with the Ethics & Compliance Initiative (ECI) to regularly survey the companies' employees about their perceptions of E&C programs and ethical culture.

- **Identify, through data and investigations, how the organizational culture contributes to misconduct.** This identification can be achieved by requiring companies to use employee surveys as critical inputs into a root cause analysis of problems that arise in the organization. For example, if employees indicate that they are uncomfortable reporting problems to management, the company should determine why the culture engenders such fear and how internal systems can be reformed to promote a speak-up culture.

  Anonymous surveys remain one of the best ways to gauge the extent to which an organization has a serious problem with fear of retaliation for reporting, for example. The DII provides its member organizations with information about their own companies as well as benchmarking data from organizations within their industries.

- **Design interventions to improve conduct and culture.** Once baseline measures are in hand, firms should be encouraged to design interventions (for example, new ways to integrate ethics goals into performance evaluations or a new policy on sales goals and compensation) and monitor how the company's culture changes over time. This is a way to determine whether targeted interventions are working and to develop a process of continual learning and experimentation. The baseline culture data can thus be used to understand the long-term impact of various internal or external initiatives at the firm.

  There is little reason to conduct extensive surveys unless the organization is open to using the revealed information to attempt to make change. In some cases, concerns about employees' reluctance to speak up, for example, have motivated organizations to create new programs based on Mary Gentile's *Giving Voice to Values* approach.[A] Subsequent surveys can help companies to assess whether they are moving the needle on this issue.

A. Gentile, M. C. (2010). *Giving voice to values: How to speak your mind when you know what's right.* New Haven, CT: Yale University Press.

interviews and focus groups, which can provide a richer sense of what it means to employees to live and work within a particular culture. If regulators, policymakers, and companies are willing to collaborate with academics to develop and validate a suite of methods for assessing ethical culture, we can together achieve the goals of the original FSGO and the vision laid out more recently by William Dudley: a business culture in which "how we do things around here" means measuring ethical culture and then trying to improve it.

author affiliation

Treviño: Smeal College of Business, The Pennsylvania State University. Haidt: New York University Stern School of Business. Filabi: Ethical Systems. Corresponding author's e-mail: afilabi@ethicalsystems.org.

endnotes

A. The Ethical Systems Culture Measurement Working Group members are Linda Treviño (Chair), Michael Brown, Jonathan Haidt, David Mayer, Marshall Schminke, Sean Stevens, Ann Tenbrunsel, Jeffrey Thomas, and Siyu Yu. Find more information about Ethical Systems at http://ethicalsystems.org.

B. To assess the ethical climate, including ethical efficacy and collective empathy, Arnaud and Schminke had respondents indicate their degree of agreement with each item of a 20-item instrument. The instrument included 10 items on the overall ethical climate (both self-interested and other interested), such as "People around here protect their own interest above other considerations." It included three items assessing ethical efficacy, such as "When necessary, people in my department take charge and do what is morally right," and seven items assessing collective empathy (also known as *collective moral emotion*), using statements such as "For the most part, when people around here see that someone is treated unfairly, they feel pity for that person."

references

1. U.S. Sentencing Commission. (1991). Chapter eight—Sentencing of organizations. Retrieved from https://www.ussc.gov/sites/default/files/pdf/guidelines-manual/1991/manual-pdf/Chapter_8.pdf

2. U.S. Sentencing Commission. (2016). 2016 Chapter 8: Chapter eight—Sentencing of organizations. Retrieved from https://www.ussc.gov/guidelines/2016-guidelines-manual/2016-chapter-8#NaN

3. Dudley, W. C. (2014). *Enhancing financial stability by improving culture in the financial services industry* [Speech transcript]. Retrieved from Federal Reserve Bank of New York website: https://www.newyorkfed.org/newsevents/speeches/2014/dud141020a.html

4. Ketchum, R. (2016, January 5). 2016 regulatory and examination priorities letter. Retrieved from Financial Industry Regulatory Authority website: http://www.finra.org/industry/2016-regulatory-and-examination-priorities-letter

5. Office of the Comptroller of the Currency. (2016). *Comptroller's handbook: Corporate and risk governance* (Version 1.0). Retrieved from https://www.occ.gov/publications/publications-by-type/comptrollers-handbook/corporate-risk-governance/pub-ch-corporate-risk.pdf

6. U.S. Consumer Financial Protection Bureau. (2016, September 4). *Consent order in the matter of Wells Fargo Bank, N.A.* (Administrative Proceeding 2016-CFPB-0015). Retrieved from http://files.consumerfinance.gov/f/documents/092016_cfpb_WFBconsentorder.pdf

7. U.S. Department of Justice, Office of Public Affairs. (2017, January 11). *Volkswagen AG agrees to plead guilty and pay $4.3 billion in criminal and civil penalties; six Volkswagen executives and employees are indicted in connection with conspiracy to cheat U.S. emissions tests* [Press release]. Retrieved from https://www.justice.gov/opa/pr/volkswagen-ag-agrees-plead-guilty-and-pay-43-billion-criminal-and-civil-penalties-six

8. Treviño, L. K., Weaver, G. R., & Reynolds, S. J. (2006). Behavioral ethics in organizations: A review. *Journal of Management, 32,* 951–989. https://doi.org/10.1177/0149206306294258

9. Shweder, R. A. (1996). True ethnography: The lore, the law, and the lure. In R. Jessor, A. Colby, & R. A. Shweder (Eds.), *Ethnography and human development* (pp. 15–52). Chicago, IL: University of Chicago Press.

10. Zimbardo, P. G. (2007). *The Lucifer effect: Understanding how good people turn evil.* New York, NY: Random House.

11. Treviño, L., & Nelson, K. (2017). *Managing business ethics* (7th ed.). Hoboken, NJ: Wiley.

12. Treviño, L. K., Weaver, G. R., & Brown, M. E. (2008). It's lovely at the top: Hierarchical levels, identities, and perceptions of organizational ethics. *Business Ethics Quarterly, 18,* 233–252. https://doi.org/10.1017/S1052150X00010952

13. Kennedy, J. A., & Anderson, C. (2017). Hierarchical rank and principled dissent: How holding higher rank suppresses objection to unethical practices. *Organizational Behavior and Human Decision Processes, 139,* 30–49.

14. Defense Industry Initiative on Business Ethics and Conduct. (n.d.). About DII. Retrieved from https://www.dii.org/about/about-dii

15. Banking Standards Board. (n.d.). What is the BSB? Retrieved from https://www.bankingstandardsboard.org.uk/what-is-the-bsb/

16. Treviño, L. K., Weaver, G. R., Gibson, D. G., & Toffler, B. L. (1999). Managing ethics and legal compliance: What works and what hurts. *California Management Review, 41*(2), 131–151.

17. Brown, M. E., Treviño, L. K., & Harrison, D. A. (2005). Ethical leadership: A social learning perspective for construct development and testing. *Organizational Behavior and Human Decision Processes, 97,* 117–134. https://doi.org/10.1016/j.obhdp.2005.03.002

18. Arnaud, A., & Schminke, M. (2012). The ethical climate and context of organizations: A comprehensive model. *Organizational Science, 23,* 1767–1780.

19. Victor, B., & Cullen, J. B. (1988). The organizational bases of ethical work climates. *Administrative Science Quarterly, 33,* 101–125.

20. Martin, K. D., & Cullen, J. B. (2006). Continuities and extensions of ethical climate theory: A meta-analytic review. *Journal of Business Ethics, 69,* 175–194.

21. Ambrose, M., & Schminke, M. (2009). The role of overall justice judgments in organizational justice research: A test of mediation. *Journal of Applied Psychology, 94,* 491–500.

22. Schoorman, F. D., & Ballinger, G. A. (2006). *Leadership, trust and client service in veterinary hospitals.* Working paper, Purdue University, West Lafayette, IN.

23. Schoorman, F. D., Mayer, R. C., & Davis, J. H. (2007). An integrative model of organizational trust: Past, present, and future. *Academy of Management Review, 32,* 344–354.

24. Ethical Systems. (n.d.). Ethics pays. Retrieved from http://www.ethicalsystems.org/content/ethics-pays

25. Guiso, L., Sapienza, P., & Zaingales, L. (2015). The value of corporate culture. *Journal of Financial Economics, 117,* 60–76.

Treating ethics as a design problem

Nicholas Epley & David Tannenbaum

abstract

Creating policies that encourage ethical behavior requires an accurate understanding of what drives such behavior. We first describe three common myths about the psychological causes of ethical behavior that can lead policymakers to overlook constructive interventions. These myths suggest that ethical behavior stems from a person's beliefs; changing behavior therefore requires changing beliefs. Behavioral science, however, indicates that the immediate context (such as an organization's norms and accepted procedures) exerts a surprisingly powerful influence on behavior. To be effective, policies must treat ethics as a design problem; that is, policymakers should create contexts that promote ethical actions. We then discuss three psychological processes that affect ethical activity—attention, construal, and motivation—and describe how understanding them can help policymakers in the public and private sectors design environments that promote ethical behavior.

Epley, N., & Tannenbaum, D. (2017). Treating ethics as a design problem. *Behavioral Science & Policy, 3*(2), 73–84.

Core Findings

What is the issue?
Policymakers commonly believe that they must first change people's beliefs in order to encourage them to adopt ethical behavior. Beyond trying to change beliefs, policymakers should also treat ethics as an environmental problem and design solutions that leverage three key psychological processes: *attention*, *construal*, and *motivation*.

How can you act?
Selected recommendations include:
1) Designing compensation strategies with prosocial goals in mind, such as tying an individual team member's bonus to group performance
2) Counteracting cognitive limitations by engaging *cognitive repair* practices such as reminders, checklists, and visible statements

Who should take the lead?
Leaders and policymakers in organizational design and human resources, behavioral science researchers, organizational psychologists

Effective policy design involves shaping human behavior. In the public sector, policymakers try to encourage some behaviors and discourage others using tools such as taxes, subsidies, mandates, bans, and information campaigns. In the private sector, policymakers try to shape behavior with tools such as hiring, firing, compensation, and operations. Policymaking therefore involves psychology—specifically, policymakers' beliefs about which levers are most effective for changing behavior. Well-intended policies can be ineffective when based on erroneous beliefs about human behavior.

Examples of failed policies based on flawed assumptions are commonplace. In 2009, for instance, the Transportation Security Administration trained more than 3,000 employees to read subtle verbal and nonverbal cues, assuming that lies would "leak out" in brief interactions. In fact, psychologists find very few reliable cues to detecting deception during ongoing interactions, and this TSA program produced a 99% false alarm rate when evaluated by the Government Accountability Office.[1] And in 2001, the U.S. government distributed $38 billion in tax rebates as part of an economic stimulus plan, based on the belief that people would spend more money when they had more to spend.[2,3] In fact, consumer spending is guided by a host of subjective evaluations about the source and meaning of money. In this case, people overwhelming saved these rebates, creating little or no short-term stimulus,[3] possibly because people interpreted the rebates as returned income rather than a windfall.[4]

Unfortunately, when it comes to considering ethical behavior, policymakers routinely hold imperfect assumptions. Common intuition presumes that people's deeply held moral beliefs and principles guide their behavior, whereas behavioral science indicates that ethical behavior also stems from momentary thoughts, flexible interpretations, and the surrounding social context. Common intuition treats the challenge of influencing ethical behavior as a problem of altering beliefs, whereas behavioral science indicates that it should also be treated as a design problem.

In this article, we describe three common myths about morality that can lead policymakers to design ineffective interventions for enhancing ethical behavior. We then discuss three basic psychological processes that policymakers in the public and private sectors can leverage when designing behavioral interventions (see Table 1). Understanding these processes can help policymakers create environments that encourage ethical behavior.

Of course, the very definition of *ethical behavior* can lead to disagreements and impasses before anyone even gets to a discussion about improving ethics. Here, we use the term to refer to actions that affect others' well-being. Ethical behavior contains some degree of prosociality, such as treating others with fairness, respect, care, or concern for their welfare. In contrast, unethical behavior contains some degree of antisociality, including treating others unfairly, disrespectfully, or in a harmful way. The inherent complexity of social behavior—which involves multiple people or groups in diverse contexts—is largely why the causes of ethical behavior can be so easily misunderstood in everyday life.

Three Myths About Morality
Common sense is based on everyday observation and guided by simplifying heuristics. These heuristics generally yield some degree of accuracy in judgment but are also prone to systematic mistakes. Comparing widely accepted common sense with the empirical record allows behavioral scientists to identify systematic errors and propose interventions for countering them.

Myth 1: Ethics Are a Property of People
All human behavior is produced by an enormously complex string of causes, but common sense often focuses on a single source: the person engaging in the activity.[5] This narrow focus can lead to a simplified belief that unethical behavior is caused by unethical people with unethical personalities—rogue traders, charlatans, or psychopaths—rather than by the broader context in which that behavior occurs.

Table 1. Myths about morality

Belief in the myths below can diminish a policymaker's ability to maximize ethical behavior.

Myth	Policy implication
Ethics are a property of people Unethical behavior is largely due to unethical individuals rather than the broader context in which behavior operates.	Can lead policymakers to overestimate the stability of ethical behavior and endorse policies to identify, detain, and deter unethical individuals (for example, "rogue traders"). Such policies are unlikely to succeed whenever unethical behavior is systemic in nature (encouraged by a "rogue" culture or industry).
Intentions guide ethical actions Good intentions lead to ethical acts, and unethical intentions lead to unethical acts. Consequently, one should infer that unethical behavior stems from unethical intentions.	Can encourage policymakers to view safeguards as unnecessary for people with good intentions, impeding implementation of sensible policies to curb unethical behavior. At times, good intentions can result in unethical behavior.
Ethical reasoning drives ethical behavior Ethical behavior is guided by deliberative reasoning based on ethical principles.	Can induce policymakers to overestimate the effectiveness of ethics training programs (standard in many organizations) and underestimate the importance of contextual changes for altering behavior.

Perhaps the best-known example of this error comes from Stanley Milgram's experiments on obedience to authority.[6] Participants in Milgram's experiments were instructed to administer increasingly severe electric shocks to another person, even to the point where participants thought the shocks might have been lethal (in fact, the "victim" was an actor who never received any shocks). When Milgram described this procedure to three different samples of people, not one person predicted that they would personally deliver the most intense electric shock possible to another person. In actuality, 65% of participants did. What makes Milgram's research so interesting is the mistaken intuition that only psychopaths or very deviant personalities would be capable of such obvious cruelty.

This myth implies that people tend to overestimate the stability of unethical behavior. Consistent with this possibility, survey respondents in one study dramatically overestimated recidivism rates—the likelihood that a past criminal would reoffend—both over time and across different crimes.[7] The likelihood of reoffending actually drops dramatically over time, but participants believed that it stays relatively constant. Participants' responses followed a rule of "once a criminal, always a criminal," a view consistent with the myth that ethical behavior is a stable property of individuals.[8] Likewise, employers who require credit checks as a precondition for employment do so because they think past defaults predict a broader tendency to engage in a wide variety of unethical behaviors (such as workplace deviance). In fact, empirical investigations have found that credit scores are, at best, weakly associated with performance appraisal ratings or termination decisions.[9,10]

Although largely unrecognized by the public, the lack of correspondence between past and future ethical behavior is not a new insight for behavioral science. A classic study in which psychologists evaluated thousands of high school and middle school students in the 1920s found very little consistency in honesty from one situation to another.[11] People tend to believe that ethical behavior reflects a consistent moral character, but actual ethical behavior varies substantially across contexts.

A focus on unethical individuals leads to policies that attempt to identify, detain, and deter those individuals (for example, "rogue traders"). This approach is unlikely to succeed whenever unethical behavior is systemic in nature (for example, it occurs within a "rogue culture" or "rogue industry"). Improving ethics often requires altering the type of situation a person is in, not simply altering the type of people in a given situation.

> "Improving ethics often requires altering the type of situation a person is in, not simply altering the type of people in a given situation"

Myth 2: Intentions Guide Ethical Actions

A more focused version of Myth 1 is the common-sense assumption that actions are caused by corresponding intentions: bad acts stem from bad intentions, and good acts follow from good intentions.[12] Although intentions are correlated with a person's actions, the relationship is far more complicated than intuitions suggest.

There are at least two consequences of over-simplifying the relationship between actions and intentions. First, people tend to overestimate the power of their own good intentions and, as a result, overestimate their propensity for engaging in ethical behavior.[13,14] People predict that they will bravely confront instances of racism, sexism, and physical abuse more often than is realistic, as such predictions fall short of the bravery people in the midst of those situations actually display.[15–17] In one experiment, for instance, 68% of women asked to anticipate how they would respond to inappropriate job interview questions posed by a male interviewer (such as "Do you have a boyfriend?") said they would refuse to answer the questions, yet none of the women did so when actually placed in that situation.[17]

Second, good intentions can lead to unintended unethical consequences simply because ancillary outcomes are overlooked.[18] People who help a friend get a job with their employer, for example, may fail to realize that this act of ingroup favoritism also harms those outside their social network.[19] Harm can therefore be done while intending to help.

Overestimating the power of good intentions can impede sensible policies to curb unethical behavior by causing people to dismiss institution safeguards as unnecessary. For instance, surveys of doctors and financial planners find that both groups think that conflict-of-interest policies are necessary for other professions but not for their own group.[20] When people think that they and their colleagues have good intentions and that people in their profession can be trusted to do what is right, they may unwisely view ethical safeguards as onerous and useless.

Myth 3: Ethical Reasoning Drives Ethical Behavior

Conventional wisdom suggests that ethical reasoning causes ethical action, but behavioral scientists routinely find that ethical reasoning also follows from behavior—serving to justify, rationalize, or explain behavior after it has occurred.[21,22] People generate sensible explanations for choices they did not make,[23] invent post hoc arguments to justify prior choices,[24] and evaluate evidence they want to believe using a lower evidentiary standard than they apply to evidence they do not want to believe.[25]

To the extent that policymakers exaggerate the causal power of ethical reasoning, they will also likely overestimate the power of ethics training programs (standard in many organizations) to change behavior. Indeed, a survey of over 10,000 representative employees from six large American companies found that the success of ethics or compliance programs was driven more by social norms within the organization than by the content of these training programs.[26]

Collectively, these three myths matter because they exaggerate the degree to which ethical behavior is driven by beliefs and can therefore be improved by instilling the right values and intentions in people. Each of the myths contains some element of truth—unethical values and intentions can at times guide unethical behaviors, and reinforcing ethical principles has some value. But these myths also oversimplify reality in a way that can lead policymakers to overlook other forces in a person's immediate context that shape ethical behavior. Policymakers who realize that encouraging ethics is not just a belief

Table 2. Ethical design principles

Ask the following questions when devising systems intended to foster ethical behavior.

Question	Policy implication
Attention: Are ethics top of mind? People have limited attention and are guided by information that is accessible, or *top of mind,* at the time a decision is made. People sometimes act unethically simply because they fail to consider the ethical implications of their behavior.	Effective systems induce people to think about ethics routinely. Examples of triggers include ethics checklists filled out before making a decision, messages that make ethical principles salient in the environment, or heuristics that can become repeated mantras for ethical action.
Construal: Are people asking, "Is it right"? How people behave is influenced by how they interpret—or construe—their environment. Altering the construal of an event can dramatically affect behavior by redefining what constitutes appropriate conduct.	Ethical systems encourage ethical construals. Inducing employees to ask themselves "Is it right?" rather than "Is it legal?" should lead to an increase increase in prosocial behavior.
Motivation: Are you using prosocial goals? Social incentives, such as a desire to help or connect with others, can be used to motivate behaviors that naturally align with ethical practices.	Systems that foster ethical behavior create opportunities for people to do good for others and highlight the good that others are doing to establish more ethical norms. Instead of focusing on ethical failures, organizations should call out *ethical beacons*—exemplary ethical behaviors—for others to emulate.

problem but also a design problem can increase ethical behavior by changing the contexts in which people live and work. Here's how.

Ethical Design for a Human Mind

For systems to be effective, they must be tailored to fit the properties of their users. Policies that encourage ethical behavior should therefore be designed around three basic psychological processes that guide human behavior: attention, construal, and motivation (see Table 2). That is, policies should be designed to help people keep ethical principles top of mind (attention), encourage people to interpret and understand the ethical ramifications of their behavior (construal), and provide opportunities and incentives to pursue ethical goals (motivation).

Attention: Make Ethics Top of Mind

Attention operates like a spotlight rather than a floodlight, focusing on a small slice of all possible relevant information. Because attention is limited, decisions are guided by whatever information is most accessible at the time the decision is made. An otherwise ethical person might behave unethically simply by failing to consider the ethical implications of his or her actions.

The limited nature of attention implies that designing environments to keep ethics top of mind should increase the likelihood of ethical behavior. In one field experiment with a U.S. automobile insurance company, customers signed an honor code either before or after completing a policy-review form that asked them to report their current odometer mileage.[27] Drivers reported their odometer reading more honestly when they signed the honor code before reporting their mileage. This kind of simple design change keeps honesty top of mind and can have a meaningful impact on a person's actions.[28]

An effective ethical system triggers people to think about ethics routinely. Such systems can include ethical checklists that are consulted before making a decision,[29] messaging that makes ethical principles salient in the environment,[30] or heuristics within an organization that can become repeated mantras for ethical action.[31] Warren Buffett, for instance, asks his employees to take the "front page test" before making any important decision: "I want employees to ask themselves whether they are willing to have any contemplated act appear the next day on the front page of their local paper—to be read by their spouses, children and friends—with the reporting done by an informed and critical reporter."[32] The key is to make sure that ethics are brought to mind by either well-learned heuristics or environmental triggers at the very time that people are likely to be contemplating an ethical decision.

Effective ethical systems can be contrasted with environments that obscure ethical considerations or chronically highlight goals that push ethics out of mind. Enron, for instance, famously had its stock price prominently displayed throughout the company, including in its elevators, whereas its mission statement, which highlighted ethical principles, was unmemorable, boilerplate, and prominently displayed nowhere in the company.[33]

Construal: Encourage People to Ask, "Is It Right?"

If you have ever watched a sporting event with a fan of the opposing team, you know that two people can witness the same event yet see very different things. How people behave is a function of how they interpret—or construe—their environment.

To understand the power of construal, consider a simple experiment in which two participants play a simple economic game.[34] In this game, both players simultaneously choose to cooperate or defect. Participants can earn a moderate amount of money if both opt to cooperate, but each player has the opportunity to earn more by defecting; however, joint defection leaves both players worse off than if both had cooperated. This task models a common tension in real-world exchanges between cooperation and exploitation. Yet simply changing the name of the game while keeping all other aspects identical (including monetary payoffs) had a dramatic impact on cooperation rates. Roughly 30% of participants cooperated when it was called the Wall Street Game, whereas 70% cooperated when it was called the Community Game. Although a name may seem like a trivial detail, altering the construal of an event can dramatically affect behavior by redefining appropriate or expected conduct for oneself and others.

At times, organizations seem to exploit the power of construal to deter ethical behavior. For instance, in the midst of serious vehicle safety concerns at General Motors, company representatives actively encouraged employees to avoid ethical interpretations of the safety issues when communicating with customers. In one illustrative case, materials from a 2008 training seminar instructed employees on euphemisms to replace ethically relevant terms when conversing with customers.[35] Instead of using the word *safety*, employees were to say, "has potential safety implications." Instead of terms with clear moral implications, employees were to use technical terminology, saying that a product was "above specifications" or "below specifications" rather than "safe" or "unsafe." Such instructions make it easier for employees to construe their behavior in ways that permit unethical behavior.

Failing to emphasize ethical construals is also where well-intentioned programs meant to ensure compliance with laws and regulations can go wrong in organizations. These programs usually focus on whether an action is legal or illegal, not whether it is ethically right. Encouraging employees to ask themselves "Is it legal?" rather than "Is it right?" could inadvertently promote unethical behavior. Andy Fastow, former chief financial officer of Enron, highlighted this disconnect when he looked back on his own acts of accounting fraud: "I knew it was wrong. . . . But I didn't think it was illegal. I thought: That's how the game is played. You have a complex set of rules, and the objective is to use the rules to your advantage."[36] As he remarked in a presentation, "The question I should have asked is not what is the rule, but what is the principle."[37] To foster ethical behavior, systems need to encourage ethical construals.

Motivation: Use Prosocial Goals

A truism of human behavior is that people do what they are incentivized to do. The challenge is to understand the specific goals that people hold at any given time and use the right kinds of incentives to shape behavior.

40

Percentage point increase in people who cooperated in a game when its name was changed from "Wall Street Game" to "Community Game"

The lost market value to a firm fined for unethical behavior relative to the fine is **$3.08 for every $1**

13%

Drop in mine injuries after requiring firms to report safety records in financial statements

"sales employees performed better after receiving a bonus to be spent on another member of their team than they did after receiving a bonus meant to be spent on themselves"

The most common approach to motivating behavior, including ethical behavior, is to provide material incentives. Although financial rewards and punishments can be productive under the right circumstances, an approach based on extrinsic incentives alone presumes that people lack meaningful prosocial motivation to begin with: to be encouraged to behave ethically, they must be compensated in some way beyond having the satisfaction of doing the right thing.

This presumption is often unwarranted. Prosocial motives, such as a desire to help or connect with others, can be used to encourage behaviors that naturally align with ethical practices. In one experiment, fundraisers at a university alumni call center worked significantly harder and raised significantly more money after having a short question-and-answer session with a beneficiary.[38] In another experiment, sales employees performed better after receiving a bonus to be spent on another member of their team than they did after receiving a bonus meant to be spent on themselves.[39] Finally, a field experiment asking one group of managers to perform random acts of kindness for employees over a 1-month period found significant reductions in depression rates among these managers 4 months after the intervention ended.[40]

The importance of social motivation can also be seen in the surprising power of social norms to shape behavior. Behavioral science repeatedly demonstrates that people mostly conform to what others around them are doing.[41] This insight can be used to motivate people for good, to the extent that ethical norms are highlighted.[42] For example, in an effort to increase tax compliance, the UK Behavioral Insights Team (at the time, a division of the British government devoted to applying behavioral science to social services) sent delinquent taxpayers letters with different messages encouraging them to pay their taxes. The most effective letter was the one informing individuals that "Nine out of ten people in the UK pay their tax on time. You are currently in the very small minority of people who have not paid us yet."[43]

The power of social norms in shaping ethical behavior has an important implication. Discussions about ethics often focus on unethical behavior—on crimes and other unethical things people are doing. Such discussions are like black holes, attracting people to them and potentially encouraging similar behavior. What is more constructive is to focus on ethical beacons—examples of admirable behavior among individuals, groups, or companies. Public service announcements, company newsletters, and other sources of information intended to encourage ethical behavior should call out exemplary ethical behavior that others can strive to emulate. To foster ethical behavior, then, policymakers should create opportunities for people to do good for others and should establish ethical norms by highlighting the good that others are already doing.

An Ethical Organization, by Design

An ethical system is an environment designed to keep ethics top of mind, make ethics central to the framing of policies and initiatives, and increase prosocial motivation. Design details must be guided by an organization's mission and by a well-crafted mission statement that features a small number of key principles. Practices, in turn, should be aligned with the stated principles as part of an organization's strategy for success. These principles must go beyond maximizing short-term shareholder value to focus, instead, on enabling long-term sustainability of the entity and its ethical actions.

Of course, policy changes inspired by an organization's core values will not produce a perfectly ethical organization, just as a well-designed bridge based on fundamental engineering principles cannot eliminate all safety risks. Ethical systems are intended to create the kind of environment that makes ethical behavior easier and therefore more frequent. At a practical level, policymakers can incorporate ethical design principles into the major drivers of behavior within their organizations: procedures for hiring and compensating employees, maintaining the entity's reputation, and carrying out day-to-day operations.

Hiring

Interviews are typically meant to identify the best person for a job, although their ability to do so is notoriously limited.[44,45] Interviews and onboarding procedures can, however, also serve as an acculturation tool that communicates an organization's ethical values to prospective employees and highlights the importance of those values to current employees.

Interviews can be designed around ethics by asking questions that make an organization's commitment to ethics clear to prospective employees. Johnson & Johnson, for instance, has a number of questions relating to its well-known credo (which pledges to prioritize the needs of the people it serves) that are put to potential employees during the interview process. For example, when discussing the company's commitment to customers, interviewers may ask potential employees to describe a time they identified and addressed an unmet customer need. Interviews designed around an organization's principles, including its ethical principles, can bring ethics to everyone's attention, encourage construal of behavior in terms of ethical principles, and signal that the organization considers ethical behavior to be an important source of motivation for both current and new employees. Even though job interviews may be poor tools for identifying and selecting the right employees, they can be used to communicate a company's values at a critical point in an employee's acculturation process. An organization that has its representatives ask about ethics during an interview signals its concern for ethics on the job.

Compensation

Organizations can design financial reward systems to encourage ethical behavior in two different ways. First, organizations can reward ethical behavior directly, such as through scorecards that translate ethical values into measurable actions. Southwest Airlines, for instance, designs its executive compensation scorecard around the company's four primary values. To reward executives for upholding the value "Every Employee Matters," the airline compensates them for low voluntary turnover. By linking compensation to keeping employees at the company, Southwest tries to create an incentive for bosses to contribute to a valuable prosocial outcome.

Second, organizations can provide opportunities for employees to satisfy preexisting prosocial motivations. People tend to feel good when they are also doing good for others,[46,47] and they also do good to maintain a positive reputation in the eyes of others.[48] Organizations can provide opportunities to satisfy both motives by allowing employees to reward one another, by facilitating random acts of kindness, or by offering employees time to engage in prosocially rewarding work that is aligned with the organization's values. In one field experiment, Virgin Atlantic rewarded its pilots for achieving a fuel-efficiency goal by giving a relatively small amount of money to the pilot's chosen charity.[49] This prosocial incentive increased pilots' reported job satisfaction by 6.5% compared with the pilots in the control condition, an increase equivalent to the observed difference in job satisfaction between those who are in poor health and those who are in good health. The good news for organizations and policymakers is that these prosocial incentives usually cost little or nothing and yet can have meaningful effects on well-being and behavior.

Reputation Management

People, including those who run organizations, care about their reputation in the eyes of others, because that reputation affects how they are treated. In one economic analysis, companies fined by the U.S. Securities and Exchange Commission for unethical behavior lost $3.08 in market share for every $1 they were fined, with these larger losses coming from the reputational consequences of being identified as a lawbreaker.[50] Policymakers who are designing ethical systems can capitalize on the reputational concerns of companies and employees to foster ethical behavior. For instance, they can ensure that an organization's reputation is measured and that the results are public and transparent.

At the individual level, many organizations already conduct annual climate or culture surveys that can be used to measure perceptions of ethical behavior within the organization. Behavioral science suggests that reporting these ethical evaluations within the organization or using them as part of the performance review process is likely to increase ethical behavior among employees, so long as making unfounded accusations can be minimized (such as when an independent agency monitors violations).

The public sector can also implement policies that enhance corporate ethics. Policies that mandate public disclosure of companies' practices often directly improve ethical behavior across an entire industry. For example, the Ministry of Environment, Lands and Parks of British Columbia, Canada, publishes a list of firms that have failed to comply with existing regulations. An empirical analysis found that publishing this list of polluters had a larger impact on subsequent emissions levels and compliance status than did fines and penalties associated with noncompliance.[51,52]

Similarly, publishing workplace safety records, thus making them more noticeable, can produce significant decreases in workplace injuries. One analysis found that a new requirement to report mine-safety records in financial statements produced an 11% drop in mine-related citations and a 13% drop in injuries.[53] Reputation systems have also been effective at increasing hygienic standards at restaurants[54] and adherence to clean drinking water standards by utility companies:[55] In Los Angeles, hygiene grading cards have caused restaurants to make hygiene improvements, and, in Massachusetts, requiring community water suppliers to inform consumers

"publishing this list of polluters had a larger impact on subsequent emissions levels and compliance status than did fines and penalties associated with noncompliance"

of violations of drinking-water regulations led to a reduction in violations. Policymakers typically focus on financial or legal incentives to shape behavior, but clearly reputational concerns can serve as a third powerful class of incentives.

Operations

Designed properly, daily operations can also offer opportunities to reinforce ethical values by keeping ethical considerations top of mind and making it easier to behave ethically. These goals can be facilitated by using organizational practices that compensate for cognitive limitations (that is, *cognitive repairs*), such as reminders, checklists, and visible statements relating to personal responsibility.[56–59]

These cognitive repairs must be timely to be effective, bringing ethical considerations to mind at the time a person is making a decision with ethical implications. One field experiment highlights the importance of timeliness. In this study, hotel valets either reminded drivers to wear their seat belt when the valet ticket was turned in (about a 6-minute delay), reminded drivers to wear their seat belt as they entered the car, or provided no reminder at all.[60] Only the immediate reminders had a noticeable impact on behavior. Drivers who received the reminder 6 minutes before starting their car were no more likely to fasten their seat belts than were drivers who received no reminder at all.

Cognitive repairs must also make the ethical consequences of one's actions obvious. In one series of experiments, researchers found that physicians were more likely to follow a standard handwashing protocol when signs at the handwashing stations reminded them about the consequences for patient safety ("Hand hygiene prevents patients from catching diseases"), compared with signs that provided instructions for handwashing or emphasized personal safety ("Hand hygiene prevents you from catching diseases").[61] The goal of these design solutions is to create an environment where ethical considerations are such a routine part of day-to-day interactions that they become automatic habits ingrained in the organization's cultural practices.

Conclusion

In writing about the 2007–2008 financial crisis, *New Yorker* reporter John Cassidy noted that he

> angered some people by suggesting that . . . [the] Wall Street C.E.O.s involved in the run-up to the financial crisis were "neither sociopaths nor idiots nor felons. For the most part, they are bright, industrious, not particularly imaginative Americans who worked their way up, cultivated the right people, performed a bit better than their

colleagues, and found themselves occupying a corner office during one of the great credit booms of all time."[62]

That this statement angered so many people illustrates how conventional wisdom often treats ethics as a belief problem: that unethical behavior is caused by individuals with unethical values or intentions.

However, the empirical evidence paints a more complicated picture: Unethical behavior is also caused by momentary thoughts, interpretations, and social context. As a result, a more accurate and constructive approach for policymakers is to treat ethical behavior as a design problem. Designing environments that keep ethics top of mind, encourage ethical construals, and strengthen prosocial motivations is essential for helping to keep otherwise good people from doing bad things.

author affiliation

Epley: University of Chicago. Tannenbaum: University of Utah. Corresponding author's e-mail: epley@chicagobooth.edu.

references

1. Government Accountability Office. (2013). *Aviation security: TSA should limit future funding for behavior detection activities* (GAO Publication No. 14-158T). Washington, DC: U.S. Government Printing Office.

2. Epley, N., & Gneezy, A. (2007). The framing of financial windfalls and implications for public policy. *Journal of Socio-Economics, 36,* 36–47.

3. Shapiro, M. D., & Slemrod, J. (2003). Consumer response to tax rebates. *American Economic Review, 93,* 381–396.

4. Epley, N., Mak, D., & Idson, L. C. (2006). Bonus or rebate? The impact of income framing on spending and saving. *Journal of Behavioral Decision Making, 19,* 213–227.

5. Gilbert, D. T., & Malone, P. S. (1995). The correspondence bias. *Psychological Bulletin, 117,* 21–38.

6. Milgram, S. (1965). Some conditions of obedience and disobedience to authority. *Human Relations, 18*(1), 57–76.

7. Vosgerau, J. (2016). *Accuracy of morality judgements.* Working paper, Bocconi University, Milan, Italy.

8. Maruna, S., & King, A. (2009). Once a criminal, always a criminal? "Redeemability" and the psychology of punitive public attitudes. *European Journal on Criminal Policy and Research, 15,* 7–24.

9. Bernerth, J. B., Taylor, S. G., Walker, H. J., & Whitman, D. S. (2012). An empirical investigation of dispositional antecedents and performance-related outcomes of credit scores. *Journal of Applied Psychology, 97,* 469–478.

10. Bryan, L. K., & Palmer, J. K. (2012). Do job applicant credit histories predict performance appraisal ratings or termination decisions? *The Psychologist-Manager Journal, 15,* 106–127.

11. Hartshorne, H., & May, M. A. (1928). *Studies in the nature of character: I. Studies in deceit.* New York, NY: Macmillan.

12. Baron, J., & Hershey, J. C. (1988). Outcome bias in decision evaluation. *Journal of Personality and Social Psychology, 54,* 569–579.

13. Epley, N., & Dunning, D. (2000). Feeling "holier than thou": Are self-serving assessments produced by errors in self or social prediction? *Journal of Personality and Social Psychology, 79,* 861–875.

14. Epley, N., & Dunning, D. (2006). The mixed blessings of self-knowledge in behavioral prediction: Enhanced discrimination but exacerbated bias. *Personality and Social Psychology Bulletin, 32,* 641–655.

15. Bocchiaro, P., Zimbardo, P. G., & Van Lange, P. A. M. (2012). To defy or not to defy: An experimental study of the dynamics of disobedience and whistle-blowing. *Social Influence, 7,* 35–50.

16. Kawakami, K., Dunn, E., Karmali, F., & Dovidio, J. F. (2009, January 9). Mispredicting affective and behavioral responses to racism. *Science, 323,* 276–278.

17. Woodzicka, J. A., & LaFrance, M. (2001). Real versus imagined gender harassment. *Journal of Social Issues, 57,* 15–30.

18. Chugh, D., Banaji, M. R., & Bazerman, M. H. (2005). Bounded ethicality as a psychological barrier to recognizing conflicts of interest. In D. A. Moore, D. M. Cain, G. Loewenstein, & M. H. Bazerman (Eds.), *Conflicts of interest: Problems and solutions from law, medicine and organizational settings* (pp. 74–95). London, United Kingdom: Cambridge University Press.

19. Bazerman, M. H., & Tenbrunsel, A. E. (2012). *Blind spots: Why we fail to do what's right and what to do about it.* Princeton, NJ: Princeton University Press.

20. Sharek, Z., Schoen, R. E., & Loewenstein, G. (2012). Bias in the evaluation of conflict of interest policies. *The Journal of Law, Medicine & Ethics, 40,* 368–382.

21. Haidt, J. (2001). The emotional dog and its rational tail: A social intuitionist approach to moral judgment. *Psychological Review, 108,* 814–834.

22. Ditto, P. H., Pizarro, D. A., & Tannenbaum, D. (2009). Motivated moral reasoning. In D. M. Bartels, C. W. Bauman, L. J. Skitka, & D. L. Medin (Eds.), *Psychology of learning and motivation: Vol. 50. Moral judgment and decision making* (pp. 307–338). San Diego, CA: Academic Press.

23. Johansson, P., Hall, L., Sikström, S., & Olsson, A. (2005, October 7). Failure to detect mismatches between intention and outcome in a simple decision task. *Science, 310,* 116–119.

24. Haidt, J., Bjorklund, F., & Murphy, S. (2000). *Moral dumbfounding: When intuition finds no reason.* Unpublished manuscript, University of Virginia, Charlottesville.

25. Dawson, E., Gilovich, T., & Regan, D. T. (2002). Motivated reasoning and performance on the Wason selection task. *Personality and Social Psychology Bulletin, 28,* 1379–1387.

26. Treviño, L. K., Weaver, G. R., Gibson, D. G., & Toffler, B. L. (1999). Managing ethics and legal compliance: What works and what hurts. *California Management Review, 41*(2), 131–151.

27. Shu, L. L., Mazar, N., Gino, F., Ariely, D., & Bazerman, M. H. (2012). Signing at the beginning makes ethics salient and decreases dishonest self-reports in comparison to signing at the end. *Proceedings of the National Academy of Sciences, USA, 109,* 15197–15200.

28. Congdon, W. J., & Shankar, M. (2015). The White House Social & Behavioral Sciences Team: Lessons learned from year one. *Behavioral Science & Policy, 1*(2), 77–86.

29. Gawande, A., & Lloyd, J. B. (2010). *The checklist manifesto: How to get things right.* New York, NY: Metropolitan Books.

30. Meeker, D., Knight, T. K., Friedberg, M. W., Linder, J. A., Goldstein, N. J., Fox, C. R., . . . Doctor, J. N. (2014). Nudging guideline-concordant antibiotic prescribing: A randomized clinical trial. *JAMA Internal Medicine, 174,* 425–431.

31. Heath, C., Larrick, R. P., & Klayman, J. (1998). Cognitive repairs: How organizational practices can compensate for individual shortcomings. *Research in Organizational Behavior, 20,* 1–37.

32. Berkshire Hathaway. (n.d.). *Berkshire Hathaway Inc. code of business conduct and ethics.* Retrieved May 25, 2017, from http://www.berkshirehathaway.com/govern/ethics.pdf

33. McLean, B., & Elkind, P. (2003). *The smartest guys in the room: The amazing rise and scandalous fall of Enron.* New York, NY: Portfolio.

34. Liberman, V., Samuels, S. M., & Ross, L. (2004). The name of the game: Predictive power of reputations versus situational labels in determining prisoner's dilemma game moves. *Personality and Social Psychology Bulletin, 30,* 1175–1185.

35. United States Department of Transportation, National Highway Traffic Safety Administration. (2014, May 16). *Consent Order TQ14-001: In re: NHTSA Recall No. 14V-047.* Retrieved from https://www.nhtsa.gov/sites/nhtsa.dot.gov/files/may-16-2014-tq14-001-consent-order.pdf

36. Elkind, P. (2013, July 1). The confessions of Andy Fastow. *Fortune*. Retrieved from http://fortune.com/2013/07/01/the-confessions-of-andy-fastow/

37. Jaffe, M. (2012, March 19). Andrew Fastow draws on Enron failure in speech on ethics at CU. *The Denver Post*. Retrieved from http://www.denverpost.com/2012/03/19/andrew-fastow-draws-on-enron-failure-in-speech-on-ethics-at-cu/

38. Grant, A. M., Campbell, E. M., Chen, G., Cottone, K., Lapedis, D., & Lee, K. (2007). Impact and the art of motivation maintenance: The effects of contact with beneficiaries on persistence behavior. *Organizational Behavior and Human Decision Processes, 103*, 53–67.

39. Anik, L., Aknin, L. B., Norton, M. I., Dunn, E. W., & Quoidbach, J. (2013). Prosocial bonuses increase employee satisfaction and team performance. *PloS One, 8*(9), Article e75509. Retrieved from https://doi.org/10.1371/journal.pone.0075509

40. Chancellor, J., Margolis, S., & Lyubomirsky, S. (2017). The propagation of everyday prosociality in the workplace. *The Journal of Positive Psychology*. Advance online publication. https://doi.org/10.1080/17439760.2016.1257055

41. Cialdini, R. B., & Goldstein, N. J. (2004). Social influence: Compliance and conformity. *Annual Review of Psychology, 55*, 591–621.

42. Nolan, J. M., Schultz, P. W., Cialdini, R. B., Goldstein, N. J., & Griskevicius, V. (2008). Normative social influence is underdetected. *Personality and Social Psychology Bulletin, 34*, 913–923.

43. Hallsworth, M., List, J., Metcalfe, R., & Vlaev, I. (2014). *The behavioralist as tax collector: Using natural field experiments to enhance tax compliance* (NBER Working Paper No. 20007). Cambridge, MA: National Bureau of Economic Research.

44. Wright, P. M., Lichtenfels, P. A., & Pursell, E. D. (1989). The structured interview: Additional studies and a meta-analysis. *Journal of Occupational Psychology, 62*, 191–199.

45. McDaniel, M. A., Whetzel, D. L., Schmidt, F. L., & Maurer, S. D. (1994). The validity of employment interviews: A comprehensive review and meta-analysis. *Journal of Applied Psychology, 79*, 599–616.

46. Andreoni, J. (1990). Impure altruism and donations to public goods: A theory of warm-glow giving. *The Economic Journal, 100*, 464–477.

47. Dunn, E. W., Aknin, L. B., & Norton, M. I. (2008, March 21). Spending money on others promotes happiness. *Science, 319*, 1687–1688.

48. Cain, D. N., Dana, J., & Newman, G. E. (2014). Giving versus giving in. *Academy of Management Annals, 8*, 505–533.

49. Gosnell, G. K., List, J. A., & Metcalf, R. D. (2017). *A new approach to an age-old problem: Solving externalities by incenting workers directly* (E2e Working Paper 027). Retrieved from E2e website: https://e2e.haas.berkeley.edu/pdf/workingpapers/WP027.pdf

50. Karpoff, J. M., Lee, D. S., & Martin, G. S. (2008). The cost to firms of cooking the books. *Journal of Financial and Quantitative Analysis, 43*, 581–612.

51. Foulon, J., Lanoie, P., & Laplante, B. (2002). Incentives for pollution control: Regulation or information? *Journal of Environmental Economics and Management, 44*, 169–187.

52. Konar, S., & Cohen, M. A. (1997). Information as regulation: The effect of community right to know laws on toxic emissions. *Journal of Environmental Economics and Management, 32*, 109–124.

53. Christensen, H. B., Floyd, E., Liu, L. Y., & Maffett, M. G. (2017). *The real effects of mandated information on social responsibility in financial reports: Evidence from mine-safety records*. Retrieved from SSRN website: https://dx.doi.org/10.2139/ssrn.2680296

54. Jin, G. Z., & Leslie, P. (2003). The effect of information on product quality: Evidence from restaurant hygiene grade cards. *The Quarterly Journal of Economics, 118*, 409–451.

55. Bennear, L. S., & Olmstead, S. M. (2008). The impacts of the "right to know": Information disclosure and the violation of drinking water standards. *Journal of Environmental Economics and Management, 56*, 117–130.

56. Heath, C., Larrick, R. P., & Klayman, J. (1998). Cognitive repairs: How organizational practices can compensate for individual shortcomings. *Research in Organizational Behavior, 20*, 1–37.

57. Haynes, A. B., Weiser, T. G., Berry, W. R., Lipsitz, S. R., Breizat, A. H. S., Dellinger, E. P., . . . Gawande, A. A. (2009). A surgical safety checklist to reduce morbidity and mortality in a global population. *New England Journal of Medicine, 360*, 491–499.

58. Rogers, T., & Milkman, K. L. (2016). Reminders through association. *Psychological Science, 27*, 973–986.

59. Zhang, T., Fletcher, P. O., Gino, F., & Bazerman, M. H. (2015). Reducing bounded ethicality: How to help individuals notice and avoid unethical behavior. *Organizational Dynamics, 44*, 310–317.

60. Austin, J., Sigurdsson, S. O., & Rubin, Y. S. (2006). An examination of the effects of delayed versus immediate prompts on safety belt use. *Environment and Behavior, 38*, 140–149.

61. Grant, A. M., & Hofmann, D. A. (2011). It's not all about me: Motivating hand hygiene among health care professionals by focusing on patients. *Psychological Science, 22*, 1494–1499.

62. Cassidy, J. (2013, August 5). Wall Street after Fabulous Fab: Business as usual. *The New Yorker*. Retrieved from https://www.newyorker.com/news/john-cassidy/wall-street-after-fabulous-fab-business-as-usual

Using behavioral ethics to curb corruption

Yuval Feldman

abstract

Even people who think of themselves as being ethical ("good people") may engage in corrupt actions. In fact, the situations that seem least problematic can sometimes cause good people to behave immorally. Behavioral ethics research has demonstrated that various unconscious and self-deceptive mental processes promote such behavior in those individuals. To reduce the frequency of misbehavior by normally well-intentioned individuals, policymakers need to be aware that classic approaches to limiting corruption sometimes increase the likelihood that good people will engage in misconduct. Regulators also need to expand their toolbox beyond formal ethical codes and financial incentives by adding preventive interventions that are based on behavioral ethics research.

Feldman, Y. (2017). Using behavioral ethics to curb corruption. *Behavioral Science & Policy, 3*(2), 87–99.

The neoclassical, rational economic view of organizational corruption lays the blame for such wrongdoing on "bad people"—self-centered individuals who consciously promote their own interests regardless of the costs to others. This view also assumes that people weigh the pros and cons of their situation and make a fully rational choice about how to behave. Further, it presumes that control of corruption depends on having formal codes of behavior; imposing high fines for misbehavior; and providing financial incentives for behaving in ways that benefit others, such as tying rewards to a group's success rather than to the actions of an individual. (See note A.)

Yet the standard approaches may fail with an important part of the population: people who see themselves as being more ethical than they really are. Behavioral ethics (BE) research demonstrates that such "good people" (as I will refer to them throughout this article) promote their own interests at the expense of others in certain situations—notably in ones that allow them to have only limited awareness of the ethical ramifications of their behavior or ones that at least enable them to deceive themselves into thinking they are behaving ethically. Ironically, at times, classical measures meant to curb corruption actually promote it.[1-14] (The ideas developed in this article are elaborated in my forthcoming book, *The Law of Good People: Challenging States' Ability to Regulate Human Behavior*). (See note B.)

Clearly, the degree to which good people act badly depends on the situation, their level of awareness of the wrongdoing, their ability to overcome unconscious processes, and their ability to find justification for noncompliance.[15,16] BE research indicates that the regulatory toolbox for curbing corruption in business needs to be expanded to address not only bad people but also bad situations that promote corrupt actions by good people. As more data are collected on the contextual factors responsible for misconduct, on the ways that situational design can change people's ethical awareness, and on the efficacy of new types of interventions, this toolbox will grow still more.

Why Good People Behave Unethically

Several psychological processes help to explain why people who usually act morally may sometimes act in their own self-interest instead of fulfilling their professional duties. As research into corruption and conflicts of interest has shown, some of these processes are unconscious. At times, for instance, corporate pressure to achieve financial goals lowers the barrier to ethical misconduct. In addition, when people do not have time to carefully consider their behavior, they rely on fast, automatic thought processes that can enable them to act unethically without reflecting on the implications of their actions.[2,17,18] (See note C.)

Furthermore, people have ethical blind spots that can prevent them from recognizing they are acting corruptly:[6] They may not realize they are doing what they want to do rather than what they should do, that they are being influenced by unconscious biases, or that they have a conflict of interest. In a corporate context, where the focus is on enhancing a company's profitability, a financial advisor might, for instance, blindly follow the firm's investment guidelines rather than fully weighing the needs of a client (to whom the advisor ethically owes loyalty).

Other psychological processes that come into play allow good people to maintain their moral image of themselves.[12] One is *motivated reasoning*, the tendency to process information in ways that fit one's self-centered desires and preexisting beliefs. Another is the tendency of people to deceive themselves, before as well as after the fact, into thinking that unethical actions are actually ethical or at least justifiable.[18] In the face of these psychological mechanisms, it can be very difficult for people to be clear on what their own motivations might actually be.[19]

The BE research has also revealed a fascinating nuance: In situations where it is easier for people to view themselves as being good, they are more likely to engage in corrupt behaviors. For example, subtle or implied gains may be more of a prod to corruption than obvious financial gains would be. Along those lines, accepting

Core Findings

What is the issue?
People overestimate how ethical they truly are. Because of various psychological processes like *motivated reasoning*, individuals are more likely to engage in corrupt behaviors when situations allow them to view themselves as being "good." Traditional interventions based on neoclassical rational assumptions may therefore inadvertently increase corruption and miss an important dimension to ethical behavior.

How can you act?
Selected recommendations include:
1) Further controlled research into corruption and nonmonetary influences like media coverage, paid speaking engagements, and conference invitations
2) Increasing the likelihood of detecting unethical behavior rather than increasing penalties for misconduct or corruption

Who should take the lead?
Regulators and industry leaders, organizational psychologists, behavioral science researchers.

gifts, which could be seen as part of a social exchange, is far easier for good people to justify than taking cash payments, which are more problematic legally and harder to justify. In that sense, the focus of law on "smoking guns" and clear quid pro quo relations completely misses the reality that it is not just bad people who behave corruptly. Focusing on finding indisputable evidence of corruption (which is needed for successful prosecution) will lead investigators to overlook all of the subtle conflicts that might affect a far greater portion of the population: the good people, for whom the subtlety of the conflict might be more, rather than less, problematic.

To understand how seeing oneself as moral can increase the likelihood of being corrupted by subtle incentives, consider what happens when a given behavior is only partly wrong. For example, public officials are not necessarily misbehaving when they vote for a given regulation, promote a certain employee, or allow a particular commercial initiative to go forward. The only factor that would make such actions corrupt is an improper motive. Promoting an employee is not problematic in itself, especially if the official doing the promoting believes the employee being given the new role is worthy. The action becomes complicated if this employee's uncle donated money to the official's campaign. In such cases, the official might have mixed motives, acting for both legitimate (the good employee deserves the job) and illegitimate (quid pro quo) reasons, and various self-serving psychological mechanisms could tip the balance toward illegitimate behavior. One such mechanism is *objectivity bias*, which causes people to downplay the effect of self-interest on their decisions and attribute their choices to legitimate motivations.[20–22] In this case, objectivity bias might cause the official to give the employee a more positive evaluation than was deserved without realizing the true source of the positive review.

In another example, a politician may convince himself that the only reason he is voting for a certain bill is because of the persuasive argument of a lobbyist rather than because of the prospect of future financial support by the interest group represented by the lobbyist. In that case, he will not be influenced by an envelope filled with cash but might be swayed by a softer influence attempt that allows him to remain convinced that he is acting objectively, not selfishly.

My colleague Eliran Halali and I discovered the force of softer incentives in a 2017 study in which participants who worked for a survey firm were themselves asked to fill out a survey reviewing a specific research institution that they hoped would later hire them to participate in additional surveys.[23] The study replicated the revolving-door effect, in which people employed in the public sector are eyeing their next job in the private sector while still working in the public sector.

Participants were asked to answer two types of questions: one type focused on the importance of the topics studied by the institution, and the other type asked the participants to evaluate the researchers at the facility. We found that participants who were told that the research institution might hire them for future work were more likely to write favorable reviews. Thus, the prospect of possible paid work did lead to an ethical bias.[23]

However, one would have expected the survey firm respondents to provide reviews that were more positive about the researchers than the topics studied, as presumably it is the researchers who are in charge of hiring decisions. Yet the participants did not give their most positive evaluations to the researchers. It seems that being blatant in the scoring might have made the participants more likely to feel that they were being unethical; they were willing to give biased reviews only to the extent that they retained an ethical self-image and did not cross some self-imposed imaginary red line. People have an internal gauge of roughly how far they will go to enhance their self-interest.[23]

Corrupting Situations
Various characteristics of work life can compound people's ability to rationalize their bad behavior. BE research indicates that

Motivated Reasoning
The tendency to process information in ways that fit one's self-centered desires and preexisting beliefs

Objectivity Bias
Downplaying the effect of self-interest on decisions and attributing choices to objective, professional, or legitimate motivations

Elastic Justification
Taking advantage of legal or situational ambiguity to rationalize self-interested behavior

"vague policies can cause employees to interpret their legal and ethical obligations loosely"

policymakers should particularly focus on the aspects described next.

Vague Rules & Norms

The view that people always behave rationally holds that vagueness in governmental or company rules deters people from attempting to find loopholes that they can exploit to their advantage.[13] The classical notion that people are averse to ambiguity likewise suggests that vagueness will deter underhanded behavior.[24] BE research demonstrates, however, that lack of specificity sometimes has the opposite effect, inducing people to use ambiguity to their advantage. Indeed, vague policies can cause employees to interpret their legal and ethical obligations loosely, especially when the policies are accompanied by weak ethical norms— that is, when people in an organization do not consistently behave in a moral way.

Maurice E. Schweitzer and Christopher K. Hsee have shown,[25] for example, that when rules are imprecise, people tend to engage in *elastic justification,* taking advantage of ambiguity to rationalize self-interested behavior.[26–31] Similarly, in experiments I conducted with Amos Schurr and Doron Teichman, subjects' interpretation of the meaning of the word *reasonable* in a hypothetical contract varied depending on how the interpretation would affect their financial gains or losses.[26] Vague legal standards were used in a self-serving way, especially when subjects had no other guidance on how they should behave.

What is more, the greater the ambiguity of a situation, the more people will feel confident in their own ethicality[32] and the more people's self-interest will take precedence over professional duties.[28,31] Conversely, reducing a person's ability to justify unethical behavior in ambiguous situations is likely to decrease the temptation for good people to misrepresent the facts.[13] Thus, regulators who wish to curb corruption through legal means should craft rules that are very specific rather than imposing general legal standards (although they should be aware of some inadvertent effects of specificity).[33]

Nonmonetary Conflicts of Interest

Policymakers usually take the rational-choice perspective and assume that financial rewards have the greatest influence on corruption and hence should be subject to the greatest scrutiny. The BE research shows the opposite effect: Nonmonetary rewards are harder to resist, especially by good people, because the motivations behind them are ambiguous and thus open to interpretation. An invitation to give a keynote speech at a conference is far more effective than cash payments at influencing many types of doctors, for instance.

Classic studies on the corrupting power of money focus on politicians influenced by campaign donations[34] and on physicians whose health care decisions are affected by the receipt of drug industry money and perks.[35] In contrast, more recent studies have analyzed situations where a government regulator has no financial ties to a private entity being regulated but does have social ties to the organization or its members, such as sharing a group identity, a professional background, a social class, or an ideological perspective.[36] In that situation, regulators were likely to treat those being regulated more leniently. Thus, even relatively benign-seeming tendencies that regulations tend to ignore—such as giving preference to people having a shared social identity—could be as corrupting as the financial ties that are so heavily regulated in most legal regimes.

In 2014, for instance, investigators in the Netherlands showed that regulators in the financial sector who had previously worked in that sector were less inclined to enforce regulations against employees who shared their background.[36,37] Similarly, in a 2013 look at the regulation of the U.S. financial industry before the 2008 crisis, James Kwak noted that the weak regulation at the time was not strictly a case of regulatory capture, in which regulatory agencies serve the industry they were meant to police without concern for the public good. Some regulators, he argued, intended to protect the public, but cultural similarities with those being regulated, such as having graduated from the same schools, prevented regulators from doing their job effectively.[38] In such instances, people often convince themselves that their responses to nonmonetary influences are legitimate, mistakenly thinking that because such influences usually go unregulated, they are unlikely to be ethically problematic.

Additional controlled research is needed on the ways that nonmonetary influences cause corruption and on how they can lead people to engage unwittingly in wrongdoing. Despite the growing recognition of the power of such influences—which might include invitations to prestigious conferences, lucrative paid speaking opportunities, or media coverage—regulators still tend to see them as less problematic than direct monetary incentives. The regulators are wrong. They need to worry about nonmonetary rewards' effects on good people at least as much as they do about the effects of financial rewards on "bad people."

Availability of Justifications

As suggested earlier, the underlying assumption of most BE approaches is that individuals want to view themselves as ethical agents. Therefore, people are more prone to unethical behavior when settings allow them to justify their actions as being ethical.[39] People who would abstain from acting out of self-interest in cases where being selfish was clearly unethical may well indulge themselves if they can easily ignore the ethical dimensions of their choices.[27,28] For example, when an organization that donates to a politician holds public views that coincide with the politician's own opinions, the politician can easily ignore the problematic nature of voting in a way that supports the donor organization.

Regulators can apply empirically tested tools to identify the common rationalizations that people use to justify corruption (such as "Everyone does it," "No one would care," or "I am not responsible"). (See note D.) Then they can take preemptive steps, perhaps by training people to recognize common justifications and informing them of the moral and legal irrelevancy of those justifications.

Loyalty to an Organization

Feeling responsible to one's company can undermine the tendency of good people to abstain from actions that can harm the company's customers, suppliers, or others. Employees are more likely to act unethically when the corporation rather than the individual benefits from the behavior and when professional norms favor unethical activity.[40] One study revealing the corrupting influence of the desire to benefit an employer showed, for instance, that when bankers were reminded of being bankers, they became less likely to behave honestly.[41] These findings run contrary to the rational-choice perspective, which holds that people are more likely to behave unethically when they themselves benefit from doing so.

Other aspects of acting on behalf of a corporation also tend to encourage unethical behavior. BE research suggests that altruism can promote corruption: People's misbehavior increases when their actions are intended to help others.[42] BE studies also indicate that in some cases, people will act more unethically when they enjoy only part of a benefit rather than all of it,[43] as happens in corporations, where revenues from misconduct are distributed among shareholders and other members of the organization.

Another characteristic of the corporate context that could increase the likelihood of good people behaving in a corrupt way is the frequent reliance on teamwork. BE research suggests that when a few people work together to execute a task, the collective nature of the endeavor can increase the chances that people will act unethically.[44]

Related findings indicate that people are more likely to engage in serious misconduct when they do it in a gradual rather than an abrupt way[45] or when they harm many unidentified victims rather than a specific individual known to them.[46] Corporations lend themselves to these kinds of situations. In many corporate contexts,

"under certain circumstances, people who work in pairs are more likely to engage in wrongdoing than if they had worked individually"

executives might also sin by omission, failing to intervene to halt the corruption of others.[47,48]

Overall, then, the corporate setting is ideal for nurturing unethical behavior in good people. Employees often do not perceive their actions as putting their own interests in front of others' and do not directly see the effects of their actions on the people—customers and others—who may be harmed. Given that unethical behavior can often benefit the corporation at the expense of the general public, regulators need to keep in mind that this environment is especially conducive to ethical violations by ordinary people.

Classic Enforcement Approaches May Inadvertently Increase Corruption

Behavioral approaches to the regulation of corruption will require new tools. Policymakers should also recognize, however, that some standard tools intended to curb corruption can actually increase it.

Disclosures

Disclosure of conflicts of interest is one of the most commonly used approaches to curbing dishonest behavior. Yet, as research by George Loewenstein and his colleagues has shown, disclosures can have paradoxical effects. For instance, although clients of financial advisors may receive worse advice from someone who has a conflict of interest, those clients may not be less trusting after reading or hearing a disclosure of that conflict of interest.[49] Research by Sunita Sah, who has analyzed the impacts of disclosures, suggests that regulators can increase the protective effects of disclosures by adjusting how the disclosures are presented.

For example, in medicine, it is best to present disclosures to patients as being mandatory rather than voluntary and best to have them delivered by a third person rather than by the doctors themselves.[50]

The Four-Eyes Principle

The *four-eyes principle*—a policy requiring that transactions be approved by two people, not just one—is well established in the corporate and political worlds. Intuitively, involvement of more people in key decisions seems as though it should reduce corruption. However, this approach can sometimes backfire, according to Ori Weisel and Shaul Shalvi, who have shown that under certain circumstances, people who work in pairs are more likely to engage in wrongdoing than if they had worked individually.[51] Their research challenges the current regulatory perspective that the four-eyes principle is an effective tool for curbing corruption.[52]

Further study is needed to understand the mechanisms underlying this surprising effect. Nevertheless, policymakers might decrease the inadvertently corrupting effects of working in dyads by making sure that each member of the pair has a different role to play and thus will not benefit in the same way from unethical behavior. Such would be the case, for instance, if one person were responsible for financial interactions with suppliers and the other person were responsible for financial interactions with clients.

Partial Solutions

When people are financially or otherwise dependent to some extent on people or organizations that could influence their ethical behavior, the effects are similar to those of nonmonetary influences. A common solution, according to the rational-choice perspective, is partial financial dependency, which should lead to less corruption than full dependency would. For example, a research center that was fully funded by only one donor would be expected to produce research results in accord with the interests of that particular donor, and the traditional solution to that dependency problem is to diversify the donor pool.

BE research on topics such as half lies[53] suggests, however, that partial dependency may create more fertile ground for corruption, because good people will have more leeway to convince themselves that the influence of any individual donor is small. Partial solutions thus provide the worst of both worlds: The problem does not go away, but good people are given the opportunity to think that it did go away, which further reduces their willingness to fight any corrupting dependency. This example translates to a larger principle: Any solution to a conflict of interest that does not eliminate the problem but only makes the conflict less blatant is likely to increase the chances that good people will behave badly.

Explicit Language in Ethical Codes

The final standard approach I discuss here is probably the most traditional: explicit ethical codes. Views about their efficacy conflict.[54] Some evidence indicates, however, that they can be made more potent by drawing on new BE approaches that combine explicit and implicit ethical interventions. For example, in a working paper on the language of ethical codes, Maryam Kouchaki, Francesca Gino, and I showed that using the word *employees* instead of *we* in an organization's ethics code was more effective in curbing employees' unethical behavior.[55] What seems to drive the effect is that the word *we* signals to employees that they are part of a community and, as such, might be forgiven for their misconduct.

Tools Inspired by BE Research

Clearly, to root out most corruption, policymakers need to revisit their regulatory toolbox and expand it to take into account the various states of mind and situations that induce good people to shirk their institutional responsibilities. The tools below can help.

Ethical Nudges

The most well-known strategy I would suggest adding to the regulatory toolbox for fighting corruption in organizations is the nudge, made famous by Richard H. Thaler and Cass R. Sunstein's book by that name.[56] Nudges are interventions that lead to behavioral changes without limiting people's free choice.

Different types of nudges have different effects and policy implications. Long-used, classical nudges are meant to remind people to act in their own self-interest and take steps meant to, say, improve their health or save money on energy bills. In contrast, ethical nudges are meant to protect third parties. They may be less effective than classical nudges, partly because the attempt to suppress a person's self-interest is likely to encounter resistance; people will not be as motivated to respond to the nudge.[57] Nevertheless, ethical nudges can be useful.

One of the best-known examples of an ethical nudge that can reduce the incidence of unethical behavior in an organizational setting is affixing one's signature to the beginning of a document rather than to its end.[58] The success of this easy, practical nudge confirms that people change their behavior when reminded of their moral responsibility at the moment of decisionmaking. Such nudges should be implemented with caution, however, because making laws that require their use—which could render them too standard or routine—might eliminate the nudges' power to remind people of their moral and professional responsibilities (an idea suggested to me by Dan Ariely).

Although the importance of nudges and other implicit measures is now recognized, policymakers should not completely toss out traditional explicit interventions. These might sometimes be more effective than implicit measures, such as for avoiding conflicts of interest. In my 2017 study with Halili, involving survey firm workers who were asked to assess a research institution that they understood might give them future work, the participants either read explicit statements about which actions are legal and moral or filled out a word-completion exercise relating to morality and deterrence of corruption before engaging in the subtle conflict-of-interest situation. We found that only the explicit messaging regarding legality and morality was effective.[23] This result is consistent with BE research showing that overt reminders to behave morally increase ethical behavior.[59]

Ways to Prevent the Corruption of Good People

Situations That Promote Corruption	Classic Solutions and Their Pitfalls	Behavioral Ethics Solutions
Vague rules and norms Ambiguity enables people who view themselves as moral to convince themselves that unethical behavior is ethical and hence legal.	**Disclosures of conflicts of interest** Ironically, delivering disclosures to customers or patients can give people license to behave in a self-interested way.	**Nudges** Nudges that frequently remind people of their ethical responsibilities may be particularly effective at promoting moral behavior. (See "Mandatory declarations" below for an example.)
Nonmonetary conflicts of interest People who would refuse outright bribes can often be swayed by more subtle rewards, such as opportunities for self-promotion.	**The four-eyes principle** Having two people approve all transactions is a widely used strategy to reduce unethical behavior, but research suggests that involvement of more people might actually increase corruption.	**Detection** Enforcement programs that invest resources in detecting corruption may be more effective deterrents than large fines (which may seem irrelevant to people who do not see themselves as behaving corruptly.)
Availability of justifications Corruption is more likely if people can convince themselves that everyone is acting in a certain way or that they are not hurting anyone.	**Partial solutions** Partial solutions (such as avoiding full dependency) could be worse than no solutions. For example, having multiple sources of funding makes it easy to feel that an ethically hazy reward provided by any one of the sources does not harm the objectivity of the funded organization.	**Blinding** Restricting access to information that might prejudice responses to other people can reduce both explicit and implicit biases.
Loyalty to an organization Feeling responsible to one's organization can reduce ethical restraints on hurting customers, suppliers, and others if doing so benefits the organization.	**Ethical codes** Such codes are widely used in organizations, but not enough attention is paid to the effects of the particular words that are used; some language choices might increase unethical behavior rather than decrease it.	**Targeted policies** Focusing on the ways that specific situations increase vulnerability to behaving unethically can be more effective than a one-size-fits-all approach.
		Mandatory declarations For corporate or government decisionmakers, frequent use of written declarations of conflicts of interest might make it harder to ignore having such conflicts.

An Emphasis on Detection

Back in 1968, Nobel laureate Gary S. Becker put forth the now-accepted notion that the effectiveness of a regulation as a deterrent to bad behavior is equal to the perception of the expected cost of being caught.[60] But BE research now challenges this equation.[31]

If, indeed, good people are not fully aware of the legal consequences of their unethical behaviors, they will be unlikely to accurately assess the benefit of that misconduct relative to its legal cost. In this regard, the BE literature supports findings from deterrence research indicating that increasing the likelihood of detection does more to prevent misconduct than increasing the size of threatened penalties does.[61] A threat of punishment can be useful, however, if it is combined with detection efforts and if the form of punishment attempts both to change the social meaning of the behavior and to convey moral norms that reinforce awareness of the ethical nature of a behavior.[62,63]

A primary focus on the magnitude of penalties, though, is particularly ill-suited to influencing the behavior of good people, who are less likely than criminals to calculate the potential punishment they might receive. Further, good people do not think that their behavior is corrupt or, at least, do not think it is as corrupt as legal policymakers would. Thus, especially when dealing with gray behaviors—the kind many of my examples have described—organizations and regulators should invest in detection rather than in increasing penalties, which assumes a calculative mind-set. (See notes E and F.)

Blinding

An important way to curb corruption related to bias is to expand efforts to disguise personal information, a strategy that is already used to avoid discrimination in employment and the justice system. In employment discrimination, this practice has been shown to be highly effective at curbing implicit biases and the unconscious effects of self-interest. In an effort to expand on that success, Christopher Robertson and Aaron Kesselheim edited a recent book on ways that blocking information might prevent unconscious biases in many institutional contexts.[64] For instance, they argue that when an expert is being paid to write an opinion about something, the expert is less likely to be biased in that opinion if he or she does not know the identity of the payer.

Use of Targeted & Integrated Policies

The motivations that drive behavior vary between people. Even good people have multiple motivations, some of which can impel them to do bad things. Two main strategies can deal with this heterogeneity and, at the same time, address people's frequent lack of awareness of their own corruption: (a) a targeted approach that is based on context-specific data collection and is tailored toward a given situation and population or (b) an integrated approach that encompasses a large number of regulatory tools and that attempts to deal with a number of different mind-sets. Each strategy has its pros and cons, and they can be used separately or together.

In the targeted, or differentiated, approach, regulations address the specific situational factors that foster corruption for particular groups. For example, regulators might need to expand their focus, not only screening bank accounts for deposits of corrupting payments but also tracking the influence of nonmonetary inducements, such as positive media coverage and prestige. In work on pharmaceutical corruption, my colleagues and I have suggested that scientists in pharmaceutical companies are

"Even good people have multiple motivations, some of which can impel them to do bad things"

often motivated by prestige and self-fulfillment; therefore, some may cut corners in their research to achieve positive results in their clinical trials of drugs. Financial fines are less relevant for this population and more appropriate for pharmaceutical executives, who might engage in misleading marketing practices to increase profits for the corporation and, hence, would be more sensitive to monetary fines.[65]

An example of the broader, integrated approach has been proposed by Shahar Ayal and his colleagues.[59] They call it REVISE, which is an acronym for REminding people not to use gray areas to justify dishonesty (by providing subtle cues that increase the salience of ethical criteria); VIsibility, or using procedures that increase people's awareness that they are being seen and recognized by other people who know them; and SElf-engagement, or reducing the gap between people's abstract perceptions of their moral self-image and their actual behavior (to keep their idealized self-image from allowing them to do wrong yet still feel that they are moral individuals). For instance, making it clear that technology is monitoring computer-based transactions should increase employees' awareness that the organization demands ethical behavior.

Mandatory Declarations Used as Ethical Reminders

A more legalistic approach to the REVISE scheme emphasizes moral reminders and uses declarations to deter misconduct that stems from people's lack of attention to their own wrongdoing and from the various self-serving mechanisms discussed above. For example, before every meeting in which executives vote, it can help to have all participants write out and sign a declaration stating that they understand the types of conflicts of interest that they need to reveal, that they do not have such conflicts, and that they know the relevant laws. Such declarations can serve two purposes. From a behavioral perspective, writing out a declaration prevents a person who wants to maintain an ethical self-image from failing to announce a conflict of interest; such omissions can be downplayed in a person's mind more than a stating an outright a lie can.[66] From a legal perspective, writing a declaration in their own handwriting reminds people that they can be prosecuted for perjury; reminders of legal consequences have been shown to be effective even for relatively subtle conflict of interests.[23]

Conclusion

In this article, I have contrasted the BE and the rational-choice accounts of the corrupted agent. Recognizing that some of the corruption in society in general and organizations in particular can be attributed to good people who view themselves as ethical and understanding the factors that cause such individuals to go astray are important for three main reasons. First, identifying the situations that enable ethical misconduct in such individuals (such as ambiguity in rules and corporate environments) can allow policymakers to alter those situations or to increase scrutiny over them. Second, the realization from BE research that some of the anticorruption tools based on rational-choice theories can have inadvertently counterproductive effects, especially on good people, can enable policymakers to be on the lookout for such effects. Finally, BE research suggests some additional tools that policymakers could use to curb corruption, such as blinding and ethical nudges. By expanding their toolbox; using a differentiated, situation-specific approach when data on a given situation exist; and using a comprehensive, integrated approach when data on specific situations are not available, policymakers will be able to make new strides in reducing corruption.

author affiliation

Feldman: Bar-Ilan University, Israel. Corresponding author's e-mail: Yuval.Feldman@biu.ac.il.

endnotes

A. For a discussion on using incentives to motivate ethical behavior in organizations, see "Reinforcing Ethical Decision Making Through Corporate Culture," by A. Y. Chen, R. B. Sawyers, and P. F. Williams, 1997, *Journal of Business Ethics, 16;* the relevant section begins on page 862.

B. Note that the "good people" scholarship is usually different from the type of research conducted by Philip Zimbardo on the Lucifer effect, which is described in *The Lucifer Effect: Understanding How Good People Turn Evil*, by P. Zimbardo, 2007, New York, NY: Random House. The "good people" research generally tries to explain how ordinary people end up doing evil or at least engaging in gross criminal behaviors.

C. For research suggesting that automaticity can lead to cooperation rather than corruption, see David G. Rand's research paradigm on this topic, as is described in the article "Social Context and the Dynamics of Cooperative Choice," by D. G. Rand, G. E. Newman, and O. M. Wurzbacher, 2015, *Journal of Behavioral Decision Making, 28,* 159–166. This argument was also recently summarized in a meta-analysis suggesting that peoples' intuition is actually more likely to lead them to be cooperative: "Cooperation, Fast and Slow: Meta-Analytic Evidence for a Theory of Social Heuristics and Self-Interested Deliberation," by D. G. Rand, 2016, *Psychological Science, 27,* 1192–1206 (https://doi.org/10.1177/0956797616654455).

D. Analogous to rationales used in the corporate setting, the rationales (for example, "It's a new era") that illegal downloaders of copyrighted files use to justify their behavior, as well as the tactics used by both copyright holders and regulators to fight these types of rationales, are reviewed in "The Law and Norms of File Sharing," by Y. Feldman and J. Nadler, 2006, *San Diego Law Review, 43,* 577–618.

E. For a review of algorithms used by different corporations to detect employees' unethical behavior when it happens rather than relying on ex post facto punishment, see "The Ethics of Intracorporate Behavioral Ethics," by T. Haugh, 2017, *California Law Review Online, 8,* https://doi.org/10.15779/Z38TD9N731.

F. For an approach that tries to separate deterrence and moral reminders, see "The Expressive Function of Trade Secret Law: Legality, Cost, Intrinsic Motivation, and Consensus," by Y. Feldman, 2009, *Journal of Empirical Legal Studies, 6,* 177–212, and "Deterrence and Moral Persuasion Effects on Corporate Tax Compliance: Findings From a Randomized Controlled Trial," by B. Ariel, 2012, *Criminology, 50,* 27–69. For a look at the effects of small punishments, see "The Effect of Unpleasant Experiences on Evaluation and Behavior," by A. Schurr, D. Rodensky, and I. Erev, 2014, *Journal of Economic Behavior & Organization, 106,* 1–9.

references

1. Feldman, Y. (in press). *The law of good people: Challenging states' ability to regulate human behavior.* Cambridge, United Kingdom: Cambridge University Press.

2. Evans, J. S. B., & Frankish, K. E. (2009). *In two minds: Dual processes and beyond.* Oxford, United Kingdom: Oxford University Press.

3. Bersoff, D. M. (1999). Why good people sometimes do bad things: Motivated reasoning and unethical behavior. *Personality and Social Psychology Bulletin, 25,* 28–39.

4. Kidder, R. M. (2009). *How good people make tough choices: Resolving the dilemmas of ethical living* (Rev. ed.). New York, NY: HarperCollins.

5. Pillutla, M. M. (2011). When good people do wrong: Morality, social identity, and ethical behavior. In D. De Cremer, R. van Dijk, & J. K. Murnighan (Eds.), *Social psychology and organizations* (pp. 353–369). New York, NY: Routledge.

6. Hollis, J. (2008). *Why good people do bad things: Understanding our darker selves.* New York, NY: Penguin.

7. Banaji, M. R., & Greenwald, A. G. (2013). *Blindspot: Hidden biases of good people.* New York, NY: Delacorte Press.

8. Banaji, M. R., & Hardin, C. D. (1996). Automatic stereotyping. *Psychological Science, 7,* 136–141.

9. Mazar, N., Amir, O., & Ariely, D. (2008). The dishonesty of honest people: A theory of self-concept maintenance. *Journal of Marketing Research, 45,* 633–644.

10. Bazerman, M. H., & Moore, D. A. (2012). *Judgment in managerial decision making* (8th ed.). Hoboken, NJ: Wiley.

11. Weber, F. J., Kurke, L. B., & Pentico, W. (2003). Why do employees steal? Assessing differences in ethical and unethical employee behavior using ethical work climates. *Business & Society, 42,* 359–380.

12. Shalvi, S., Gino, F., Barkan, R., & Ayal, S. (2015). Self-serving justifications: Doing wrong and feeling moral. *Current Directions in Psychological Science, 24,* 125–130.

13. Feldman, Y., & Smith, H. E. (2014). Behavioral equity. *Journal of Institutional and Theoretical Economics, 170,* 137–159.

14. Zamir, E., & Sulitzeanu-Kenan, R. (2016, November 29). *Explaining self-interested behavior of public-spirited policymakers* (Hebrew University of Jerusalem Legal Research Paper No. 17-8). Retrieved November 2017 from SSRN website: https://ssrn.com/abstract=2876437

15. Shalvi, S., Eldar, O., & Bereby-Meyer, Y. (2012). Honesty requires time (and lack of justifications). *Psychological Science, 23,* 1264–1270.

16. Bazerman, M. H., & Gino, F. (2012). Behavioral ethics: Toward a deeper understanding of moral judgment and dishonesty. *Annual Review of Law and Social Science, 8,* 85–104.

17. Haidt, J. (2001). The emotional dog and its rational tail: A social intuitionist approach to moral judgment. *Psychological Review, 108,* 814–834.

18. Moore, D. A., & Loewenstein, G. (2004). Self-interest, automaticity, and the psychology of conflict of interest. *Social Justice Research, 17,* 189–202.

19. Hochman, G., Glöckner, A., Fiedler, S., & Ayal, S. (2015). "I can see it in your eyes": Biased processing and increased arousal in dishonest responses. *Journal of Behavioral Decision Making, 29,* 322–355.

20. Armor, D. A. (1998). The illusion of objectivity: A bias in the perception of freedom from bias. *Dissertation Abstracts International: Section B. The Sciences and Engineering, 59*(9-B), 5163.

21. Pronin, E., Gilovich, T., & Ross, L. (2004). Objectivity in the eye of the beholder: Divergent perceptions of bias in self versus others. *Psychological Review, 111,* 781–799.

22. Chugh, D., Bazerman, M. H., & Banaji, M. R. (2005). Bounded ethicality as a psychological barrier to recognizing conflicts of interest. In D. A. Moore, D. M. Cain, G. Loewenstein, & M. H. Bazerman (Eds.), *Conflicts of interest: Challenges and solutions in business, law, medicine, and public policy* (pp. 74–95). Cambridge, United Kingdom: Cambridge University Press.

23. Feldman, Y., & Halali, E. (2017). Regulating "good" people in subtle conflicts of interest situations. *Journal of Business Ethics.* Advance online publication. https://doi.org/10.1007/s10551-017-3468-8

24. Nagin, D. S. (1998). Criminal deterrence research at the outset of the twenty-first century. *Crime and Justice, 23,* 1–42.

25. Schweitzer, M. E., & Hsee, C. K. (2002). Stretching the truth: Elastic justification and motivated communication of uncertain information. *Journal of Risk and Uncertainty, 25,* 185–201.

26. Feldman, Y., Schurr, A., & Teichman, D. (2013). Reference points and contractual choices: An experimental examination. *Journal of Empirical Legal Studies, 103,* 512–541.

27. Bazerman, M. H., Loewenstein, G., & Moore, D. A. (2002). Why good accountants do bad audits. *Harvard Business Review, 80*(11), 96–103.

28. Feldman, Y., & Harel, A. (2008). Social norms, self-interest and ambiguity of legal norms: An experimental analysis of the rule vs. standard dilemma. *Review of Law & Economics, 4,* 81–126.

29. Moore, D. A., Tetlock, P. E., Tanlu, L., & Bazerman, M. H. (2006). Conflicts of interest and the case of auditor independence: Moral seduction and strategic issue cycling. *Academy of Management Review, 31,* 10–29.

30. Cain, D. M., Loewenstein, G., & Moore, D. A. (2010). When sunlight fails to disinfect: Understanding the perverse effects of disclosing conflicts of interest. *Journal of Consumer Research, 37,* 836–857.

31. Feldman, Y., & Teichman, D. (2009). Are all legal probabilities created equal? *New York University Law Review, 84,* 980–1022.

32. Dana, J., Weber, R. A., & Kuang, J. X. (2007). Exploiting moral wiggle room: Experiments demonstrating an illusory preference for fairness. *Economic Theory, 33,* 67–80.

33. Boussalis, C., Feldman, Y., & Smith, H. E. (2017). Experimental analysis of the effect of standards on compliance and performance. *Regulation & Governance.* Advance online publication. https://doi.org/10.1111/rego.12140

34. Lessig, L. (2011). *Republic, lost: How money corrupts Congress—and a plan to stop it.* New York, NY: Twelve.

35. Dana, J., & Loewenstein, G. (2003). A social science perspective on gifts to physicians from industry. *JAMA, 290,* 252–255.

36. Jones, D. (2000). Group nepotism and human kinship. *Current Anthropology, 41,* 779–809.

37. Veltrop, D., & de Haan, J. (2014). *I just cannot get you out of my head: Regulatory capture of financial sector supervisors* (De Nederlandsche Bank Working Paper No. 410). Retrieved from https://papers.ssrn.com/sol3/papers.cfm?abstract_id=2391123

38. Kwak, J. (2014). Cultural capture and the financial crisis. In D. Carpenter & D. A. Moss (Eds.), *Preventing regulatory*

capture: Special interest influence and how to limit it (pp. 71–98). New York, NY: Cambridge University Press.

39. Shalvi, S., Dana, J., Handgraaf, M. J., & De Dreu, C. K. (2011). Justified ethicality: Observing desired counterfactuals modifies ethical perceptions and behavior. *Organizational Behavior and Human Decision Processes, 115,* 181–190.

40. Kouchaki, M. (2013). *Professionalism and moral behavior: Does a professional self-conception make one more unethical?* (Edmond J. Safra Working Paper No. 4). Retrieved from https://dx.doi.org/10.2139/ssrn.2243811

41. Cohn, A., Fehr, E., & Maréchal, M. A. (2014, December 4). Business culture and dishonesty in the banking industry. *Nature, 516,* 86–89.

42. Gino, F., Ayal, S., & Ariely, D. (2013). Self-serving altruism? The lure of unethical actions that benefit others. *Journal of Economic Behavior & Organization, 93,* 285–292.

43. Wiltermuth, S. S. (2011). Cheating more when the spoils are split. *Organizational Behavior and Human Decision Processes, 115,* 157–168.

44. Soraperra, I., Weisel, O., Kochavi, S., Leib, M., Shalev, H., & Shalvi, S. (2017). The bad consequences of teamwork. *Economics Letters, 160,* 12–15.

45. Gino, F., & Bazerman, M. H. (2009). When misconduct goes unnoticed: The acceptability of gradual erosion in others' unethical behavior. *Journal of Experimental Social Psychology, 45,* 708–719.

46. Amir, A., Kogut, T., & Bereby-Meyer, Y. (2016). Careful cheating: People cheat groups rather than individuals. *Frontiers in Psychology, 7,* Article 371. https://doi.org/10.3389/fpsyg.2016.00371

47. Pittarello, A., Rubaltelli, E., & Motro, D. (2016). Legitimate lies: The relationship between omission, commission, and cheating. *European Journal of Social Psychology, 46,* 481–491.

48. Libson, A. (2016). *Directors' conflict-of-interest impact on passive behavior: Evidence from directors on the Tel-Aviv stock exchange.* Manuscript in preparation.

49. Cain, D. M., Loewenstein, G., & Moore, D. A. (2005). The dirt on coming clean: Perverse effects of disclosing conflicts of interest. *The Journal of Legal Studies, 34,* 1–25.

50. Sah, S., Loewenstein, G., & Cain, D. M. (2013). The burden of disclosure: Increased compliance with distrusted advice. *Journal of Personality and Social Psychology, 104,* 289–304.

51. Weisel, O., & Shalvi, S. (2015). The collaborative roots of corruption. *Proceedings of the National Academy of Sciences, USA, 112,* 10651–10656.

52. Irlenbusch, B., Mussweiler, T., Saxler, D., Shalvi, S., & Weiss, A. (2016). *Similarity increases collaborative cheating.* Unpublished manuscript.

53. Fischbacher, U., & Föllm-Heusi, F. (2013). Lies in disguise—An experimental study on cheating. *Journal of the European Economic Association, 11,* 525–547.

54. O'Fallon, M. J., & Butterfield, K. D. (2005). A review of the empirical ethical decision-making literature: 1996–2003. *Journal of Business Ethics, 59,* 375–413.

55. Kouchaki, M., Feldman, Y., & Gino, F. (2017). *The ethical perils of codes of conduct in a personal, informal language.* Unpublished manuscript.

56. Thaler, R. S., & Sunstein, C. (2008). *Nudge: Improving decisions about health, wealth, and happiness.* New Haven, CT: Yale University Press.

57. Feldman, Y. (2014). Behavioral ethics meets behavioral law and economics. In E. Zamir & D. Teichman (Eds.), *Oxford handbook of behavioral economics and the law* (pp. 213–240). New York, NY: Oxford University Press.

58. Shu, L. L., Mazar, N., Gino, F., Ariely, D., & Bazerman, M. H. (2012). Signing at the beginning makes ethics salient and decreases dishonest self-reports in comparison to signing at the end. *Proceedings of the National Academy of Sciences, USA, 109,* 15197–15200. https://doi.org/10.1073/pnas.1209746109

59. Ayal, S., Gino, F., Barkan, R., & Ariely, D. (2015). Three principles to REVISE people's unethical behavior. *Perspectives on Psychological Science, 10,* 738–741.

60. Becker, G. S. (2000). Crime and punishment: An economic approach. In N. G. Fielding, A. Clarke, & R. Witt (Eds.), *The economic dimensions of crime* (pp. 13–68). London, United Kingdom: Palgrave Macmillan. (Original work published 1968)

61. Klepper, S., & Nagin, D. (1989). The deterrent effect of perceived certainty and severity of punishment revisited. *Criminology, 27,* 721–746.

62. Mulder, L. B. (2016). When sanctions convey moral norms. *European Journal of Law and Economics.* Advance online publication. http://doi.org/10.1007/s10657-016-9532-5

63. Feldman, Y. (2009). Expressive function of trade secret law: Legality, cost, intrinsic motivation, and consensus. *Journal of Empirical Legal Studies, 6,* 177–212.

64. Robertson, C. T., & Kesselheim, A. S. (Eds.). (2016). *Blinding as a solution to bias: Strengthening biomedical science, forensic science, and law.* London, United Kingdom: Academic Press.

65. Feldman, Y., Gauthier, R., & Schuler, T. (2013). Curbing misconduct in the pharmaceutical industry: Insights from behavioral ethics and the behavioral approach to law. *The Journal of Law, Medicine & Ethics, 41,* 620–628.

66. Spranca, M., Minsk, E., & Baron, J. (1991). Omission and commission in judgment and choice. *Journal of Experimental Social Psychology, 27,* 76–105.

editorial policy

Behavioral Science & Policy (BSP) is an international, peer-reviewed publication of the Behavioral Science & Policy Association and Brookings Institution Press. BSP features short, accessible articles describing actionable policy applications of behavioral scientific research that serves the public interest. Articles submitted to BSP undergo a dual-review process: For each article, leading disciplinary scholars review for scientific rigor and experts in relevant policy areas review for practicality and feasibility of implementation. Manuscripts that pass this dual-review are edited to ensure their accessibility to policy makers, scientists, and lay readers. BSP is not limited to a particular point of view or political ideology.

Manuscripts can be submitted in a number of different formats, each of which must clearly explain specific implications for public- and/or private-sector policy and practice.

External review of the manuscript entails evaluation by at least two outside referees—at least one in the policy arena and at least one in the disciplinary field.

Professional editors trained in BSP's style work with authors to enhance the accessibility and appeal of the material for a general audience.

Each of the sections below provides general information for authors about the manuscript submission process. We recommend that you take the time to read each section and review carefully the BSP Editorial Policy before submitting your manuscript to *Behavioral Science & Policy*.

Manuscript Categories

Manuscripts can be submitted in a number of different categories, each of which must clearly demonstrate the empirical basis for the article as well as explain specific implications for (public and/or private-sector) policy and practice:

- Proposals (≤ 2,500 words) specify scientifically grounded policy proposals and provide supporting evidence including concise reports of relevant studies. This category is most appropriate for describing new policy implications of previously published work or a novel policy recommendation that is supported by previously published studies.
- Reports (≤ 3000 words) provide a summary of output and actionable prescriptions that emerge from a workshop, working group, or standing organization in the behavioral policy space. In some cases such papers may consist of summaries of a much larger published report that also includes some novel material such as meta-analysis, actionable implications, process lessons, reference to related work by others, and/or new results not presented in the initial report. These papers are not merely summaries of a published report, but also should provide substantive illustrations of the research or recommendations and insights about the implications of the report content or process for others proposing to do similar work. Submitted papers will undergo BSP review for rigor and accessibility that is expedited to facilitate timely promulgation.

- Findings (≤ 4,000 words) report on results of new studies and/or substantially new analysis of previously reported data sets (including formal meta-analysis) and the policy implications of the research findings. This category is most appropriate for presenting new evidence that supports a particular policy recommendation. The additional length of this format is designed to accommodate a summary of methods, results, and/or analysis of studies (though some finer details may be relegated to supplementary online materials).
- Reviews (≤ 5,000 words) survey and synthesize the key findings and policy implications of research in a specific disciplinary area or on a specific policy topic. This could take the form of describing a general-purpose behavioral tool for policy makers or a set of behaviorally grounded insights for addressing a particular policy challenge.
- Other Published Materials. BSP will sometimes solicit or accept *Essays* (≤ 5,000 words) that present a unique perspective on behavioral policy; *Letters* (≤ 500 words) that provide a forum for responses from readers and contributors, including policy makers and public figures; and *Invitations* (≤ 1,000 words with links to online Supplemental Material), which are requests from policy makers for contributions from the behavioral science community on a particular policy issue. For example, if a particular agency is facing a specific challenge and seeks input from the behavioral science community, we would welcome posting of such solicitations.

Review and Selection of Manuscripts

On submission, the manuscript author is asked to indicate the most relevant disciplinary area and policy area addressed by his/her manuscript. (In the case of some papers, a "general" policy category designation may be appropriate.) The relevant Senior Disciplinary Editor and the Senior Policy Editor provide an initial screening of the manuscripts. After initial screening, an appropriate Associate Policy Editor and Associate Disciplinary Editor serve as the stewards of each manuscript as it moves through the editorial process. The manuscript author will receive an email within approximately two weeks of submission, indicating whether the article has been sent to outside referees for further consideration. External review of the manuscript entails evaluation by at least two outside referees. In most cases, Authors will receive a response from BSP within approximately 60 days of submission. With rare exception, we will submit manuscripts to no more than two rounds of full external review. We generally do not accept re-submissions of material without an explicit invitation from an editor. Professional editors trained in the BSP style will collaborate with the author of any manuscript recommended for publication to enhance the accessibility and appeal of the material to a general audience (i.e., a broad range of behavioral scientists, public- and private-sector policy makers, and educated lay public). We anticipate no more than two rounds of feedback from the professional editors.

Standards for Novelty

BSP seeks to bring new policy recommendations and/or new evidence to the attention of public and private sector policy makers that are supported by rigorous behavioral and/or social science research. Our emphasis is on novelty of the policy application and the strength of the supporting evidence for that recommendation. We encourage submission of work based on new studies, especially field studies (for Findings and Proposals) and novel syntheses of previously published work that have a strong empirical foundation (for Reviews).

BSP will also publish novel treatments of previously published studies that focus on their significant policy implications. For instance, such a paper might involve re-working of the general emphasis, motivation, discussion of implications, and/or a re-analysis of existing data to highlight policy-relevant implications or prior work that have not been detailed elsewhere.

In our checklist for authors we ask for a brief statement that explicitly details how the present work differs from previously published work (or work under review elsewhere). When in doubt, we ask that authors include with their submission copies of related papers. Note that any text, data, or figures excerpted or paraphrased from other previously published material must clearly indicate the original source with quotation and citations as appropriate.

Authorship

Authorship implies substantial participation in research and/or composition of a manuscript. All authors must agree to the order of author listing and must have read and approved submission of the final manuscript. All authors are responsible for the accuracy and integrity of the work, and the senior author is required to have examined raw data from any studies on which the paper relies that the authors have collected.

Data Publication

BSP requires authors of accepted empirical papers to submit all relevant raw data (and, where relevant, algorithms or code for analyzing those data) and stimulus materials for publication on the journal web site so that other investigators or policymakers can verify and draw on the analysis contained in the work. In some cases, these data may be redacted slightly to protect subject anonymity and/or comply with legal restrictions. In cases where a proprietary data set is owned by a third party, a waiver to this requirement may be granted. Likewise, a waiver may be granted if a dataset is particularly complex, so that it would be impractical to post it in a sufficiently annotated form (e.g. as is sometimes the case for brain imaging data). Other waivers will be considered where appropriate. Inquiries can be directed to the BSP office.

Statement of Data Collection Procedures

BSP strongly encourages submission of empirical work that is based on multiple studies and/or a meta-analysis of several datasets. In order to protect against false positive results, we ask that authors of empirical work fully disclose relevant details concerning their data collection practices (if not in the main text then in the supplemental online materials). In particular, we ask that authors report how they determined their sample size, all data exclusions (if any), all manipulations, and all measures

in the studies presented. (A template for these disclosures is included in our checklist for authors, though in some cases may be most appropriate for presentation online as Supplemental Material; for more information, see Simmons, Nelson, & Simonsohn, 2011, *Psychological Science, 22, 1359–1366*).

Copyright and License

Copyright to all published articles is held jointly by the Behavioral Science & Policy Association and Brookings Institution Press, subject to use outlined in the *Behavioral Science & Policy* publication agreement (a waiver is considered only in cases where one's employer formally and explicitly prohibits work from being copyrighted; inquiries should be directed to the BSPA office). Following publication, the manuscript author may post the accepted version of the article on his/her personal web site, and may circulate the work to colleagues and students for educational and research purposes. We also allow posting in cases where funding agencies explicitly request access to published manuscripts (e.g., NIH requires posting on PubMed Central).

Open Access

BSP posts each accepted article on our website in an open access format at least until that article has been bundled into an issue. At that point, access is granted to journal subscribers and members of the Behavioral Science & Policy Association. Questions regarding institutional constraints on open access should be directed to the editorial office.

Supplemental Material

While the basic elements of study design and analysis should be described in the main text, authors are invited to submit Supplemental Material for online publication that helps elaborate on details of research methodology and analysis of their data, as well as links to related material available online elsewhere. Supplemental material should be included to the extent that it helps readers evaluate the credibility of the contribution, elaborate on the findings presented in the paper, or provide useful guidance to policy makers wishing to act on the policy recommendations advanced in the paper. This material should be presented in as concise a manner as possible.

Embargo

Authors are free to present their work at invited colloquia and scientific meetings, but should not seek media attention for their work in advance of publication, unless the reporters in question agree to comply with BSP's press embargo. Once accepted, the paper will be considered a privileged document and only be released to the press and public when published online. BSP will strive to release work as quickly as possible, and we do not anticipate that this will create undue delays.

Conflict of Interest

Authors must disclose any financial, professional, and personal relationships that might be construed as possible sources of bias.

Use of Human Subjects

All research using human subjects must have Institutional Review Board (IRB) approval, where appropriate.